Pierre Elliott Trudeau

Richard Gwyn

Fitzhenry & Whiteside

Contents

THE CANADIANS ® *A Continuing Series*

Pierre Elliott Trudeau

© 2006 Richard Gwyn

Fitzhenry & Whiteside Limited, 195 Allstate Parkway, Markham, Ontario L3R 4T8

www.fitzhenry.ca   godwit@fitzhenry.ca

Fitzhenry & Whiteside acknowledges with thanks the Canada Council for the Arts and the Ontario Arts Council for their support of our publishing program. We acknowledge the financial support of the Government of Canada through the Book Publishing Industry Development Program (BPIDP) for our publishing activities.

 Canada Council Conseil des Arts
for the Arts du Canada

 ONTARIO ARTS COUNCIL
CONSEIL DES ARTS DE L'ONTARIO

Library and Archives Canada Cataloguing in Publication

Gwyn, Richard, 1934-

Pierre Elliott Trudeau / Richard Gwyn.

(The Canadians)

Includes index.

ISBN 1-55041-774-6

1. Trudeau, Pierre Elliott, 1919-2000. 2. Canada—Politics and government—1963-1984. 3. Prime ministers—Canada—Biography. I. Title. II. Series: Canadians.

FC626.T7G993 2005   971.064'4'092   C2004-906965-9

Cover illustration: John Mardon

Layout: Darrell McCalla

Printed and bound in Canada

Introduction

Seldom has there been a political leader so complex, so impossible to predict, so difficult to understand, so private and yet so public, as Pierre Elliott Trudeau, elected Canada's prime minister four times between 1968 and 1984.

At every turn, the man displayed contradictions.

His dismissive shrug. The biting wit. The affection he lavished on his three young sons, two of them born on Christmas Day.

The prime ministerial swimming pool paid for by anonymous corporate donors. His impassioned proclamation of an international doctrine of "sharing."

The sleek silver-grey Mercedes. The rose in his lapel. The gunslinger pose he invented—thumbs thrust into his belt and feet splayed far apart. The magic of marriage to a young "flower child."

The fierce intimacy of his friendships, as with Gérard Pelletier, his lifelong intellectual and moral mentor. The cool distance between himself and every aide who worked closely with him for years but whose first names he could never remember.

Pierre Trudeau would plunge naked into a lake or swimming pool amid strangers of both sexes. As minister of justice, he enacted liberal legislation on divorce, homosexual relations, and abortion. And yet most Canadians did not realize until his funeral, on October 3, 2000, that Trudeau was extremely religious, going regularly to mass and attending retreats year after year where he re-examined himself and deepened his faith.

Yes, Pierre Trudeau was difficult to figure out. As a close friend of his remarked, "He guards his ambiguity jealously."

Even his political policies could seem unpredictable. He came to power convinced that government had to do more with less. In his first year he actually reduced the size of the civil service, the branches of government administration. By the end of his term, however, he had involved the government in areas where it had never been before.

He had put in place economic policies such as wage and price controls, and he had set up the Foreign Investment Review Agency. In fact, he was widely condemned as a quasi-socialist.

Trudeau was free of prejudice and a true supporter of multiculturalism. But, surprisingly, his policy of encouraging multiculturalism in Canada (for which he came to be most strongly praised) did not take root because of his personal conviction in its value for its own sake. He introduced it because it was strategic, a ploy to win support for English and French bilingualism, which some ethnic groups originally opposed.

Amid all these contradictions, Trudeau also displayed unwavering convictions. For his entire life, Trudeau detested nationalism—the belief that nations should act independently, emphasizing their own goals rather than international ones—regarding it as a step backward, even destructive for society. He battled to the limit and beyond for official bilingualism in Canada, regarding it as a right owed to, and possessed by, French-speaking Canadians, as one of Canada's founding peoples. He saw it as a national necessity to help prevent the separation of Quebec from the rest of the country. Trudeau also relentlessly pursued the Charter of Rights and Freedoms for Canada, convinced that protecting their rights would free Canadians to find themselves, excel, and turn Canada into "a role model for the world."

Perhaps he was the least Canadian of all our prime ministers, with such "non-Canadian" characteristics as a capacity for ruthlessness, a lifelong fascination with Eastern spiritualism, and a lack of interest in Canada's overwhelming neighbour, the United States. Yet Canadians came to embrace him as they had no other leader since Wilfrid Laurier, prime minister from 1896 until 1911. By the time of his death, the achievements Trudeau had established for Canada—the Charter of Rights and Freedoms, a federal policy of multiculturalism, a federal policy of official bilingualism, a federal recognition of equality of the provinces with no special status for Quebec, an international policy of peacekeeping and "human security"—had become an inseparable part of the country. In fact, to English-speaking Canadians especially, they *were* Canada. The Canada of the twenty-first century is Trudeau's Canada.

Chapter 1
Early Days: Family and School

Pierre Trudeau didn't have any of the experiences that often shape an exceptional individual. He didn't have an unhappy childhood, he wasn't hardened by financial hardship (a chauffeur drove him to his private school), and there was no great scholar, explorer, or artist among his ancestors to serve as a role model. His exceptionality came entirely from within himself and from his family. "My father taught me order and discipline, and my mother, freedom and fantasy," Trudeau said.

For nearly three centuries, the Trudeaus were farmers in Quebec. It was Pierre's father, Charles-Emile (known simply as Charles) Trudeau, who broke the mould. A short, slight man, bold, boisterous, and authoritarian, he was a lover of athletics. From his father, Pierre learned to pursue excellence, especially in athleticism. Although not a natural athlete, Pierre became an exceptional swimmer, diver, boxer, and canoeist.

Charles-Emile began his professional life as a lawyer and subsequently launched himself as a businessman, at the time an unusual step for a French Canadian. Charles built up a string of automobile service stations and sold these to Imperial Oil. He then invested in a baseball club, in mining and real estate, and even financed some professional boxers. He experienced incredible success, becoming a multimillionaire.

St. James Street, Montreal, about 1920. Montreal was Canada's largest city when Pierre Trudeau was growing up.

Charles married into the élite. His wife, Grace Elliott, was English-speaking and Anglo-Saxon. Soft-voiced, refined, graceful, and delicate, she was also made of steel. "Formidable" is the word those who knew her used most often. She and Charles-Emile had three children, Suzette, Pierre Elliott in 1919, and Charles. Pierre would live with his mother until he was 41, and even as prime minister he called his mother almost every day. Pierre once said about his mother, "She left her children free," and it is to her that he attributes his absolute commitment to personal freedom.

Charles-Emile died at a young age, passing on his wealth to his three children. His father's early death was a devastating blow to 15-year-old Pierre. He had adored his father—and feared him. Ever afterward he cried at funerals. Ever afterward he deeply respected authority, but constantly challenged it.

Clearly, Trudeau was born to wealth and privilege, the son of two Canadians, and wholly bilingual, which was uncommon at the time. His life was entwined with the worlds of both the French and the English. All his early schooling was in French. Through cousins, he got to know rural Quebec and to be at ease with its *joual* (or slang), and his closest friends—Gérard Pelletier, Jacques Hébert, Jean LeMoyne, and Jean Marchand—were all francophone. When Pierre eventually married, he did so to a unilingual anglophone.

Trudeau took one step toward becoming someone exceptional when, at the age of 12, he became a student at Collège Jean de Brébeuf in Montreal. The school was run by Jesuits, members of a Roman Catholic order who imbued their students with a sense of being special and with a conviction that will and discipline could conquer all. Their curriculum was extraordinary. One of Trudeau's teachers, Père Robert Bernier, has described some of it: "Literature, philosophy, music, painting—all went together … I taught them French, Greek and Latin literature … outside of class we would read and discuss in English authors like Hemingway, Faulkner, Henry James, Hawthorne and Thoreau … We could easily enter the mind of philosophers and historians such as Locke, de Tocqueville, Acton, Jefferson."

Trudeau learned facts, dates, theories, and philosophical ideas during his eight years at Brébeuf, but, more importantly, he learned how to learn. His ferocious mental discipline dates from these years. Here was the basis for his lifelong commitment to always reading a book right through, never skipping a chapter, a paragraph, a sentence. It was here that he began to hone his memory, which became razor sharp, providing him with the ability to unnerve opponents in later political debates by quoting some unwise remark they'd once made.

Trudeau's lifelong Catholicism was also a legacy from his years at the Jesuit-run college of Brébeuf. He was not a conventional Catholic, however. Trudeau once said: "I believe in the Protestant rule of conscience and that you must not deliberately hurt others. That's the only sin." He was strongly influenced by a system of thought called Personalism, which was developed in France in the 1930s. It supported social activism, such as the worker-priests. Personalism went against traditional Catholic views by suggesting that Catholics could interpret Church doctrine for themselves without having to blindly follow the hierarchy. One of Trudeau's top political aides, Tom Axworthy, sums up the importance in Trudeau's life and actions of both his ideas and his beliefs with this comment: "You cannot understand Pierre Trudeau unless you understand him as a Catholic intellectual."

Lastly, it was at Brébeuf that Trudeau acquired a passionate, lifelong attachment to that great hero of French literature, Cyrano de Bergerac, the swordsman, wit, poet, and adventurer. To the end of his days, Trudeau would talk about Cyrano's famous declaration:

> To sing, to laugh, to dream
> To walk in my own way …
> And if my nature wants that which grows
> Towering to heaven like the mountain pine,
> I'll climb, not high perhaps, but all alone.

So Trudeau set off to climb, alone.

Chapter 2
Searching for a Cause

Pierre Trudeau's climbing took some interesting twists and turns. When he graduated from Collège Jean de Brébeuf in 1940, he studied law at the University of Montreal, passing his bar exams in 1944. Then he went to Harvard University, in Massachusetts, to study for a master's degree in political economy. He hung a sign on his door: "Pierre Trudeau, Citizen of the World." In 1946 Trudeau headed to Paris, France, to study at the Sorbonne. In 1947 he went to London, England, to study at the London School of Economics.

Trudeau during a visit to the Middle East, 1949

Then, in 1948, he was ready to travel the world. Even by today's round-the-world standards, his year-long tour was remarkable. He went from Germany to Eastern Europe to the Balkans to Turkey, to the Middle East, Afghanistan, India, Burma, Indo-China, and China. He met the local people, travelling in a turban or a burnoose, sometimes living on goat's milk and honey. He worked as a missionary with the Holy Cross Fathers in (what is now) Bangladesh. In Jerusalem and then in Belgrade, he was arrested as a spy. In China, he ate raw sea slugs. He came back knowing more about the world than most Canadians.

When he landed back in Canada, Pierre Trudeau was 30 years old. Others had started careers. He was still searching for a cause.

Gérard Pelletier, a young, idealistic intellectual, found it for him. They were attracted to each other because both were politically progressive—unusual in Quebec at the time. Pelletier had founded a new magazine, *Cité Libre*, that dared to challenge the leadership of Quebec's premier, Maurice Duplessis. Duplessis was the leader of the Union Nationale, a conservative provincial party. He had ruled the province almost as a dictator since 1944, in alliance with the Roman Catholic Church and many foreign (mostly American) corporations.

Maurice Duplessis

Duplessis represented the traditional French-Conservative nationalism, rooted in the Church and in the countryside. The *Cité Libre* staff and supporters were liberals and social democrats, and although all were passionate Quebecers, they were really internationalists. Trudeau was persuaded to write for the magazine. His writing was brilliant and cutting. For example, he dismissed all francophone federal politicians since Confederation (with the exception of Laurier) as irrelevant to Canada's evolution, comparing them to "witch doctors" who pretended they could affect people's lives.

Trudeau continued to write for *Cité Libre* for a decade, developing a coherent critique of Quebec politics as it was being run by the right-wing, nationalist Duplessis government and the Church. Outside Quebec, and certainly today, his ideas would not seem particularly extreme. He insisted on democracy, on the right of people to express themselves freely and to freely form associations, such as unions. He wanted an end to political corruption and patronage. He preached the need for "functionalism," advocating that the federal government and the provinces each pursue the activities best suited to them. He insisted on the importance of social justice and of respect for the rule of law.

Because the province was being governed so repressively, Trudeau's ideas seemed radical, even extremist. In fact, in 1950s

Quebec, it was virtual communism—and at that time, it could be very risky, even dangerous, to be accused of supporting communism. Trudeau was refused a professorship at the University of Montreal, and Gérard Pelletier's wife, Alex, recalled, "Very few would talk to us."

Trudeau with his friends Jean Marchand and Gérard Pelletier

Trudeau was expressing his ideas and beliefs in print, but he felt writing wasn't enough. Inspired by Pelletier, and also by the labour leader Jean Marchand, he moved beyond words and into action. He joined the miners in the famous strike at Asbestos in 1949. To escape the claustrophobia of conservative, Church-dominated Quebec, Trudeau spent two years in Ottawa working in the Privy Council Office, the administrative body at the very centre of the federal government that serves the prime minister and coordinates the activities of the Cabinet.

Then, suddenly, in 1959, things changed in Quebec, not because of *Cité Libre*, nor because of Trudeau, but because Duplessis died. The deep freeze that had gripped the province for so many years suddenly began to melt. The University of Montreal invited Trudeau to become a professor of law. A year later, the Union Nationale party, which Duplessis had headed, was defeated and a Liberal government was elected in Quebec. It was led by former federal Cabinet minister Jean Lesage. With him came an entirely new crop of activist democrats, like René Lévesque and Eric Kierans, and, as top aides, Jacques Parizeau and Claude Morin.

The "Quiet Revolution" was beginning. This period of reforms in many areas within the province, including social, economic, and educational, lasted from 1960 to 1966 and brought with it the first stirrings of a new Quebec nationalism. The new politicians wanted their provincial government to play a larger role in all decision making. They had complete confidence that the provincial government could do more for Quebecers than the federal government could in distant Ottawa. In 1962, Lesage won a second election with the provocative slogan, "Maîtres Chez Nous" (masters in our own house), a reference to this policy of provincial control over provincial matters. This was a virtual declaration of war on Ottawa.

Jean Lesage

At this time, Trudeau was still outside of Quebec, working in Ottawa at the Privy Council Office. He was now criticized, by many members of Quebec's cultural élite of academics and journalists, for being a dilettante, always driving around in his Mercedes with a succession of beautiful women. He was considered clever, certainly, but rich and spoiled. Over 40 years of age, he was also in danger of becoming out of date. Instead of being attacked as too liberal, he was accused of being insufficiently "nationalist." Trudeau would not give an inch, stating that Quebec had to come "out of its wigwam." In 1961 he warned: "Open the borders. This people is dying of asphyxiation." In 1962 he wrote an article, "The New Treason of the Intellectuals," damning the French-Canadian élite for abandoning ordinary people by using Quebec nationalism—and the new jobs it created for them in the provincial government—to serve their own career interests.

Mostly on his own, but helped by old friends like Pelletier and Marchand and by new ones like Marc Lalonde and a rising Ottawa civil servant, Michael Pitfield, Trudeau began developing a critique of Quebec's new nationalism. His fullest expression of it was in his famous 1965 essay in *Cité Libre*, "Federalism and the French-Canadians." He wrote: "It is not the concept of the nation that is retrograde. It is the idea that the nation must necessarily be sovereign."

Trudeau advocated federalism, a system in which the provinces are united under a federal government. The federal government has some power; the provinces have other powers. Different peoples or nations could be distinctive and yet form a larger whole. No province has greater powers than the others. Trudeau believed that if one province, such as Quebec, had greater powers than the others, it would gradually inch its way toward outright sovereignty, rejecting the authority of the federal government. Further, argued Trudeau, if each province tried to become sovereign, other nations within the province could likewise claim independence, so that there would be no end to the process. Sovereignty instead should reside with the individual. A person should be free to be whatever he or she wishes to be. Each Canadian should be protected from the arbitrary power of the state by a bill of rights.

Trudeau also called, perhaps idealistically, for "participatory democracy," in which all citizens involved themselves more directly in their own governance.

Trudeau was unusual, not just in Canada, but in any western democracy; he was a potential leader with a clearly thought-out set of ideas. At 30, he had been searching for a cause, and he had found it. Now he had to find a way to put his ideas into action.

Various changes had been taking place in Canada over many years, but it was in the mid-1960s that they coalesced to create a new kind of country and society. The new Canada was urban, and cities like Montreal, Toronto, and Vancouver were becoming metropolitan and culturally sophisticated. Cultural centres and art galleries began sprouting up, and universities expanded enormously. Canada's ties with Britain, the mother country, had withered away and were being replaced by a cross-border intimacy that a new breed of English-Canadian nationalists found threatening because of the immense power of the United States. Expo '67, the world's fair that was held in Montreal in 1967, brought an incredible 50 million visitors to that city. Canadians, unused to international recognition for anything other than hockey and growing wheat, were unbelieving when the event drew praise from the rest of the world for its stylishness, cleverness, artistry, and its modernity. For the first time ever, Canada was acknowledged as world class.

At first, Pierre Trudeau crept into this new scene at its outer margins. Prime Minister Lester Pearson wanted new Quebec recruits for the 1965 election to replace those who had had to resign because of a series of scandals. He sought out Marchand, an influential labour leader, and Pelletier, a highly regarded journalist. They insisted they would only run if their buddy Trudeau was invited to as well. Dubbed "The Three Wise Men," all three won seats—Trudeau most easily of all in the heavily anglophone riding of Mount Royal in Montreal.

Prime Minister Lester Pearson soon made Trudeau his parliamentary secretary and then, in an amazingly quick jump, his minister of justice. Pierre impressed and surprised everyone by working ferociously hard at his new responsibilities. On December 5, 1965, he presented a bill, "An Act Respecting Divorce," in which the old, repressive rules that determined the causes for divorce were scrapped and replaced by a simple declaration of

Prime Minister Pearson with his minister of justice, Pierre Elliott Trudeau, 1968

Searching for a Cause

"marriage breakdown." Two weeks later he introduced comprehensive reforms of the Criminal Code. At that time, both abortions and homosexual acts were illegal. Trudeau's reforms, among other matters, permitted therapeutic abortions (abortions performed for the physical or mental health of the pregnant woman) and, astonishingly for those times, legalized homosexuality. He responded to critics with the famous phrase, "The state has no place in the bedrooms of the nation."

In politics, luck and timing can be almost everything. Just at the moment when Trudeau burst onto the national scene, Prime Minister Pearson announced he would be leaving politics. Soon the Liberals would have to pick a new leader. Pearson presided over a constitutional conference in Ottawa where Trudeau, as justice minister, defended the federalist position against Quebec Premier Daniel Johnson. They argued before the television cameras, Trudeau articulating, with skill and scorn, the federalist principles he'd proclaimed in *Cité Libre*, and Johnson arguing back for special status for Quebec. Trudeau clearly won the exchange, described as "perhaps the most spectacular duel in Canadian politics." It made Trudeau the darling of English Canada, of the media, and of young people. He was tough, brainy, sexy, and witty. He personified the new Canada of Expo '67. Above all, he was unbeatable on television. Marshall McLuhan, the great communications guru, pronounced that he had the right "mask"—a "charismatic mask"—for that medium.

Political rivals Pierre Trudeau and John Turner

The race for leader began, and Trudeau, although unknown, immediately became the front-runner. He stayed in front, and it quickly became inevitable that Trudeau would win the leadership and become prime minister. He had everything, even the best lines. As he himself said, it was time for "new guys with new ideas." When the last ballot result was announced, Trudeau had won 1,203 votes; Robert Winters, 954; and John Turner, 195. Trudeau plucked the rose from his lapel and tossed it into the adoring crowd.

Pierre Elliott Trudeau wins the Liberal Party leadership in 1968 and becomes prime minister of Canada

The federal election was set for June 25, 1968, and its result seemed just as inevitable. Trudeau's campaign became a giant national love-in. His theme of "The Just Society," while undefined, caught the public's fancy. The Liberal Party's theme song was "To Dream the Impossible Dream" from the musical, *The Man from LaMancha*. Trudeau inspired Canadians to dream as they never had before—of being excellent, of having a leader the world admired, of doing things in a different, exciting way.

At the annual Jean Baptiste Day parade in Montreal, some rowdy people infiltrated the crowd and began throwing bottles at the reviewing stand where the dignitaries, including Pierre Trudeau, were watching the parade. All the dignitaries fled to safety—all but Trudeau. He sat, impressively unflinching, and untouched.

Trudeau won an easy majority, from coast to coast. In April 1968 he was sworn in as prime minister. He then appointed those close to him, such as Marc Lalonde and Michael Pitfield, to senior posts in his office. He shuffled the Cabinet, moving some people in and out of ministerial positions. And then he disappeared.

Chapter 3
Just Watch Me

Few prime ministers have come to office with higher public expectations than Pierre Trudeau—and then so completely disappointed people. Part of the problem was that the expectations were so exaggerated. Canadians projected onto Trudeau their desires and dreams, which were often contradictory. For example, they wanted him to keep Quebec quiet and fulfill Quebecers' hopes for a bilingual Canada. Often the expectations were downright impossible, such as an instant end to unemployment and poverty.

Another part of the problem was that, although Trudeau had thoughts about how he wanted to handle a few core issues, such as bilingualism and constitutional reform, he had no other ideas about what he wanted to do with the power that was now his.

Finally, Trudeau hated being what he had become, a politician and the country's leader. He loved being free, as he had been all his life, to do whatever he wanted, and he did not want to conform to anyone's idea of what a statesman should be. He continued to defy authority—even though he *was* now that very authority. Trudeau pirouetted behind the Queen on a trip to London where they met at the Commonwealth head office at Marlborough House. He dismissed elected members of Parliament as "nobodies," and he told political journalists they were "a crummy lot." Then, on March 4, 1971, he married a young woman, Margaret Sinclair, a "flower child," who did not fit the traditional mould of a prime minister's wife.

Canadians did see Trudeau accomplishing some useful things. The government was reorganized and a new Department of

Regional Economic Expansion was created. Reforms were put in place to make Parliament more efficient. Innovative new programs were set up to promote community and social development and to reach out to young people (such as the Company of Young Canadians). A constitutional task force was created to consider changes to Canada's founding document, the British North America Act. Above all, legislation was enacted to promote bilingualism within the civil service and to enable all French- and English-speaking Canadians to be served in the language of their choice within federal institutions. Efforts were made to increase the number of francophones in senior positions in the public service.

Pierre Trudeau on a skating date with Margaret Sinclair, 1970

This was all admirable stuff. But because Trudeau so hated being a politician, he made no effort to sell bilingualism across the country. Instead he left that task to Gérard Pelletier. But Pelletier lacked the communication skills for the job, so it wasn't done effectively. Trudeau's first love was being an intellectual. He made just one change when he moved into the prime minister's official residence at 24 Sussex Drive. In the stairwell he hung a quilt made by artist Joyce Wieland into which she'd patchworked the phrase so associated with him: *la raison avant la passion*/reason before passion.

Academics, thinkers, and intellectuals poured into Ottawa and mixed with high-minded civil servants and brainy backroom aides to study all of the nation's problems and to arrive at cool and clear solutions to them. Buzz phrases, such as "management by objective," were honoured as if they were holy words. Out of all this talk, however, there came almost no action. For one entire afternoon, for example, the Cabinet debated the difference between "public aspirations" and "public expectations"; no conclusions were reached. A cumbersome review of foreign policy was undertaken and resulted in no change in foreign policy at all. And so it went, in almost every sphere of government. During Trudeau's first four years as prime minister, critics agreed almost unanimously, he had missed a great chance to change the nation.

Unfortunately, however, government action of serious and dramatic proportions was demanded during the autumn of 1970. Here, Trudeau did fulfill the exaggerated expectations that Canadians had of him. He waged a war against terrorists dedicated to the destruction of Canada. And he won, hands down.

It was mid-morning, Monday, October 5, 1970. Radio and television stations interrupted their regular programming and released a shocking news bulletin. A British trade commissioner, James Cross, had been seized at his Westmount home in Montreal by four young men. In a note, they described them-

Trudeau entertains John Lennon and Yoko Ono in Ottawa, 1969

selves as members of the Liberation Cell of the Front de Libéra-
tion du Québec (FLQ). They threatened to execute Cross unless
they were given $500,000 in gold bullion and 23 jailed members
of the FLQ were released.

For a week, little happened. The government rejected the
kidnappers' demands, but the federal and Quebec governments
did initiate negotiations. As a gesture of good intent, they
allowed the FLQ Manifesto, a declaration of the organization's
principles, to be read on national television. These principles
were hard to understand, but it was clear they called for separation and/or a socialist state. To the surprise of the authorities,
many of the statements in the Manifesto, such as its description
of Quebec as "a society of terrorized slaves," were supported by
the Quebec public. Most people, in fact, treated the affair as a
bit of a lark.

The following Saturday, October 15, Quebec Labour
Minister Pierre Laporte was kidnapped while playing ball outside
his Montreal home. The kidnappers described themselves as
belonging to the Chenier Cell. Suddenly everything changed.
One kidnapping could be a fluke; two had to be a large-scale
conspiracy. Support for the FLQ grew as Quebecers began to
realize that it might be a major new political force. Three thou-
sand students and workers gathered at a public rally. That same
day, Trudeau's Cabinet met and approved the enactment of the
War Measures Act. In Canada, police cannot normally detain
and interrogate suspects without charging them. The War
Measures Act permits them to do just that. It was, in effect,
national martial law.

The FLQ's Chenier Cell reacted by strangling Laporte. The
police discovered his body in the trunk of his own car at St.
Hubert air base. His funeral was held at Notre Dame Cathedral
in Montreal three days later.

With the death of Laporte, the FLQ lost all public support.
Effectively, the crisis was over. Without public support the small
number of terrorists were bound to be captured by the authorities. Five hundred suspects were taken in by police under the
War Measures Act, but they were released quickly; fewer than a

dozen were ever convicted. On December 2, 1970, police surrounded a house in north Montreal. They had found Cross and his kidnappers. Negotiations granted the Liberation Cell members safe conduct to Cuba in exchange for the release of Cross. (After going from Cuba to France, the four eventually returned to Canada.) On December 28, the three remaining members of the murderous Chenier Cell were arrested without any bloodshed at a farm south of the city. All were sentenced to long prison terms, and after serving their time, were eventually released.

Trudeau's handling of the FLQ crisis most defined his first term as prime minister. He had been forced to confront a kind of domestic terrorism that was unknown in Canada, and scarcely known in any western democracy at that time. His response to the crisis made a large impression on Canadians, whether they approved of what he did or not.

Many believed that he acted as a hero, remaining cool and determined as he faced down the terrorists and preserved social stability. When asked by a journalist how far he would go to pursue the killers, he uttered his now famous tough-guy line, "Just watch me." Two days later, he invoked the War Measures Act. The majority of Canadians supported the tough way in which he

A helicopter and Canadian soldiers stand ready at Quebec Provincial Police headquarters in Montreal to deal with FLQ attacks in 1970.

Trudeau talks to the press during the FLQ crisis

dealt with the kidnappers. To many, this decision destroyed his reputation as a champion of civil liberties.

The War Measures Act turned into an administrative disaster as well as a moral one. Most of the people arrested were harmless intellectuals, artists, and unionists. But Trudeau never showed the smallest doubts. He dismissed as "bleeding hearts" those who protested the appearance of armed soldiers on the streets of Ottawa and Montreal. Eric Kierans, a Liberal minister, described Trudeau's performance as "very cold, very tough, totally determined. It was very, very impressive."

Margaret, in her memoir, reveals Trudeau's tenderness as she recalled her husband's inconsolable sobbing after learning of Laporte's death. And yet, right after the discovery of Laporte's body, Prime Minister Trudeau went on national television and declared, "Through justice, we shall defend our values, our order, and our laws. Through justice, we shall rid ourselves of perversion and terrorism." He ended, in the French version, by announcing, "Nous vaincrons!" (We will win!), brilliantly claiming for the Canadian government the boastful words of the FLQ's famous slogan.

During the FLQ crisis of 1970, Canadians saw their prime minister apply his skill, toughness, and ruthlessness to the cause of defeating violence. Along the way he unquestionably breached the rules of civil liberties that he himself had preached his entire life. And yet, like his character, his prime ministerial record is contradictory. The leader who, in 1970, angered civil libertarians more than any other prime minister in modern times, would in the years following expand Canadian civil liberties more widely than in all the years before him by enacting the Charter of Rights and Freedoms.

Chapter 4

Margaret and MacEachen

During his first four years as prime minister, Trudeau challenged authority repeatedly, but the authority he kept challenging was his own. Canadians began to wonder whether Trudeau simply wasn't up to the job of running the country. Perhaps he was a dilettante (the term he hated most) who had lucked his way into office. To many, he certainly seemed to have been wasting a lot of time and the opportunity to make significant changes.

A federal election was coming up. From the beginning, his campaign was a disaster. The Liberal slogan, "The Land is Strong," had been widely mocked as meaningless. Trudeau's high-minded, ultra-rationalist speeches had gone over the heads of ordinary Canadians.

Election day came on Monday, October 30, 1972, and Trudeau underwent an experience utterly novel to him. In the full view of the public, he was humiliated and thrashed—and almost lost. When the ballots were counted, the Liberals had won just 109 seats, only 2 more than the 107 won by the Conservatives, led by Robert Stanfield. The New Democrats had won 31 seats, and 17 seats were scattered among the other parties. Only sheer luck saved Trudeau from being defeated and forced out of public life after a single term. It seemed enough that Quebecers had voted for the Liberal Party—not in support of Trudeau's policies or mandates, but mainly as an expression of their "tribalism" and nationalism, the very concepts that Trudeau deplored—to squeak him back into power. Trudeau had been given another chance to prove himself.

For several weeks Trudeau went into something close to a depression. To add to his gloom, many of the French Canadians around him put his poor showing down to an English-Canadian "backlash" against bilingualism.

One of Trudeau's greatest gifts as a leader was never to indulge in self-pity or in wishful thinking. He wasted no time and lost no sleep on might-have-beens. After a brief bout of pessimism—one of the few times that he had succumbed to it—he was soon back on track, coolly considering what had happened and then figuring out what he had to do about it. And he came to a key conclusion: if he wanted to gain the support of Canadians, reason could no longer come before passion. As Trudeau told a television interviewer in December 1973, "Nine-tenths of politics ... appeals to emotion rather than to reason. I'm a bit sorry about that, but this is the world we are living in, and therefore I've had to change."

The prime minister didn't merely change himself—he transformed himself. At the age of 53, Trudeau reinvented himself, dedicating himself to becoming a politician. Trudeau realized he had to win back the Liberal Party and the Canadian people. So he finally got busy.

Out from his office went the intellectuals; in came a crowd of practised Liberal politicians, such as Jim Coutts, Keith Davey, Jerry Grafstein, and Royce Frith. He himself criss-crossed the country meeting with Liberal supporters and, for the first time ever, invited them to dinners at his home at 24 Sussex Drive.

Trudeau started making all the right political gestures. Bilingualism was downplayed. He had once made an irreverent pirouette behind the Queen's back and offended many Canadians who respected her; now she was invited to Canada, not once, but twice. He suddenly emerged as a friend of English-Canadian nationalists, creating the Foreign Investment Review Agency (FIRA) to review foreign takeovers of Canadian companies. He also enacted a national energy policy that included a subsidized national oil price (to Alberta's fury) and a national energy corporation (again to Alberta's fury). Both moves expanded Ottawa's power deep into provincial jurisdictions. The legislative record of his 1972–74 government has few equals in modern Canadian politics in terms of new policies enacted.

Allan MacEachen, a canny, gloomy Scot, was an experienced Cabinet minister whom Trudeau had previously ignored. Now Trudeau made an extremely important choice to appoint him as House Leader. Because the Liberals were a minority government with only two seats more than the Progressive Conservative Party, all votes in Parliament were close. This meant that the 48 votes held by the other parties were extremely important; if the other parties wanted to, they could vote together with the Conservatives and defeat the Liberals, thereby toppling Trudeau's government.

One thing MacEachen did was to keep contentious legislation out of the House of Commons for as long as possible so that the possibilities of Liberal defeat were minimized. He courted David Lewis, a former labour lawyer and leader of the New Democratic Party (NDP). The NDP, with its block of 31 votes, was key to the government's survival. MacEachen urged Trudeau to consider pursuing measures that the NDP approved of and would vote for. The Liberal budget of February 1973 threw money in all the directions the NDP wanted, from higher pensions to higher children's allowances.

The Conservatives denounced the "unholy alliance" but could do nothing. By the fall of 1973, Trudeau had bounced back in the polls, and he was receiving praise from the press. In December, Trudeau announced the national energy policy; its goal was "before the end of this decade, Canadian self-sufficiency in oil." The NDP, and the English-Canadian nationalists, applauded.

Trudeau was winning in Parliament. But he wanted a majority government so that he no longer had to depend on the support of the NDP, and to get that, he needed an election. He began taunting the NDP, calling the members "seagulls, squawking and squealing above the ship of state, and pretending to steer it." The Liberals proposed a budget that slashed taxes to the middle class. To Trudeau's great relief, the NDP voted against it, and the budget was defeated. Too late, Lewis realized that he had handed

Trudeau, now popular in the polls, the opportunity to try again for a majority government. The election was on.

"In 1972 my campaign never really got off," said Trudeau early in the campaign. "This year I've found the secret. I have a train ... And I have Margaret." By travelling with him everywhere, waving and smiling and sometimes making a few direct and sincere remarks ("He taught me all about loving"), Margaret softened the tough prime minister and made him human to the public. With her beside him, he became the kind of person ordinary people could relate to.

Margaret campaigns for Trudeau in 1974

Pierre Trudeau and Margaret Sinclair had met in December 1967 in Tahiti. Trudeau had gone there to think about running for the Liberal leadership. Instead, after a meeting by the pool, he found himself thinking constantly about the violet-eyed, 23-year-old daughter of a former Liberal Cabinet minister, James Sinclair. Margaret came to Ottawa. They dated secretly, then openly. They married in Vancouver in March 1971.

Pierre Trudeau was the leader of the Liberal Party and one of the most sought-after bachelors in the world. Margaret was beautiful and fun, a flower child in the era of peace and love. By 1974, the couple had two sons, Justin, born in 1971, and Alexandre (Sasha), born in 1973. Their third son, Michel, was born in 1975.

For a time, they enjoyed their life together, but it all ended abruptly. Settled into 24 Sussex Drive, Margaret soon discovered

Pierre and Margaret with Justin and Sasha

that Trudeau was no fun at all. He was a highly disciplined workaholic. Each night, Trudeau went through his Cabinet papers. He expected Margaret to entertain herself. Once, when Margaret asked what she should do, he told her to read Ovid (an eighth-century Roman poet). He was a true, self-contained loner who seemed to need no one.

But it was not until later that all the hurt and anger would burst out. In 1972 Margaret, innocent and guileless, beautiful, and so loving, was a major asset to Trudeau's campaign.

Trudeau became, in fact, too good a politician. A sad truth about elections is that it is much easier to persuade people to vote *against* something, a person or a policy, than *for* something. As soon as Trudeau understood this, he applied it ruthlessly. Inflation is a general increase in prices. In Canada, it had

climbed uncomfortably high. Conservative leader Robert Stanfield announced during the campaign that he planned to introduce a policy of wage and price controls to control inflation. Trudeau was relentless in his ridicule. "Zap, you're frozen," he told his audiences. Wage and price controls were "a disaster waiting to happen." The only thing they actually could control "will be your wages," Trudeau warned. His comments were clever and he excelled at attacking Stanfield, but he didn't come up with a counter-proposal. Inflation was a serious problem that was eating away at the economy. After the election, whoever was elected prime minister would have to find a way to solve it.

Robert Stanfield

On July 8, 1974, Canadians gave back to Trudeau his majority and their trust. At the ballroom of the Chateau Laurier Hotel in Ottawa, Trudeau beckoned to his side the two people who had contributed the most to his triumph—Margaret and his minister of finance, John Turner. Within little more than a year, both of them would be gone.

Chapter 5
The Sun King

Right after the 1974 election, Robert Stanfield, the Progressive Conservative leader, announced his resignation; his successor was bound to be new and untried. Effectively, no opposition to Pierre Trudeau existed any longer. Among the provincial premiers, only P.E.I's Alex Campbell had been in office longer than Trudeau, and only a few of his Cabinet ministers had more experience than he did. On the world scene, Trudeau was now the senior leader in the G–7, the association formed by the seven leading industrial nations. He could do almost anything he wanted. But just as things were looking good, things went badly wrong—on many fronts.

Things went wrong for Trudeau personally. Late in 1974, Margaret entered a hospital in Montreal "for observation," telling reporters she'd had a nervous breakdown. The next year, accompanying her husband on a trip to South America, she smoked marijuana in public in Cuba, and at a state dinner in Venezuela, she made an impromptu speech, ending in a song. The following March

Pierre and Margaret with Fidel Castro (holding Michel) in Cuba

she spent her sixth wedding anniversary in Toronto without her husband. She attended a Rolling Stones concert, stayed at the same hotel as the popular rock group, and made remarks in a magazine interview that Trudeau, and much of the public, found jarringly personal. After returning home, she appeared in public with a black eye. There was speculation as to whether or not it was given to her by Trudeau.

In May 1977, the Trudeaus issued a short statement saying, "they shall be living separate and apart. Margaret relinquishes all privileges as the wife of the Prime Minister ... Pierre will have custody of their three sons, giving Margaret generous access to them."

Things also went wrong for Trudeau in terms of his political image. He returned to his former flamboyant style, the style that Canadians had rejected when they voted in the 1972 election. Immediately after the 1974 election, Trudeau allowed his friends to organize a fundraising campaign to build an indoor swimming pool at 24 Sussex Drive. Next came a $30,000, armour-plated, silver-grey Cadillac as the official prime ministerial car. After that, he received large sums to refurbish his parliamentary office and 24 Sussex Drive, including $8,200 for a sofa. He also brought back the type of aides, such as Michael Pitfield, that he had removed during his minority government. The Cabinet became more and more of an empty shell, and he increasingly became an imperial prime minister, governing not with the assistance of elected ministers and members of Parliament, but with his personal aides and a small number of civil service officials. Media commentators began calling him the "Sun King," after France's grandiose Louis XIV.

Things also went wrong for Trudeau in terms of party politics. Finance Minister John Turner was his most admired Cabinet minister—handsome, athletic, fluently bilingual, intelligent, outgoing, and likeable. But as Trudeau's economic policies became increasingly interventionist, Turner found himself less and less listened to as he tried to explain the concerns of the business community. After a meeting with Trudeau in September 1975, Turner resigned from the government. Once Turner was gone—and with him, his pro-business viewpoint—support for the Trudeau government from business people, and increasingly from Canadians in all walks of life, plummeted.

And things also went wrong for Trudeau in terms of national politics. In Quebec in the fall of 1976, René Lévesque swept to office at the head of his pro-separatist Parti Québécois.

As well, there were major problems with the Canadian economy. Two days after the 1974 election, Statistics Canada reported that inflation had topped 11.4 per cent, its highest level in 25 years. Interest rates also went into double digits. Inflation is a problem for a country because it causes a general increase in prices and a decrease in the purchasing value of money. Trudeau's response to the problem was to do virtually nothing. When the Throne Speech, which outlines the government's legislative agenda, was delivered that autumn in the House of Commons, it called the problem "serious and urgent" but offered no solutions.

René Lévesque, leader of the Parti Québécois

To many, the solution was obvious. Everyone, from conservative C.D. Howe Institute economists to Canadian-born liberal economist John Kenneth Galbraith, was urging the government to impose controls on wages and prices. The belief was that limiting the amounts by which wages and prices could increase would limit the rise of inflation.

The Sun King

But Trudeau had a difficulty with this solution. He'd spent the 1974 election ridiculing Stanfield's support for controls and making extravagant claims that his government had "wrestled inflation to the ground." How could he now put in place wage and price controls?

When John Turner quit Trudeau's government, he solved the prime minister's problem for him. Trudeau had no choice now. He could deal with inflation—or watch his government fall apart.

Trudeau moved quickly, appointing one of his best ministers, Donald Macdonald, to the finance portfolio and making wage and price controls the government's top, and only, priority. The prime minister announced the scheme to institute wage and price controls on national television on October 13, 1976. "We have to swallow strong medicine … to cool the fires of inflation," he said. Increase in both prices and wages—by all government agencies and some 1,500 private firms—would be regulated by a new national board. These controls would remain for three years.

The unions and the business community turned against him, and the pro-business western provinces, especially Alberta, were outraged.

Despite a lot of mix-ups and red tape, polls showed that Canadians supported controls from the start. But they didn't support Trudeau's version of controls. He couldn't bring himself to say he had been wrong to oppose controls, nor to apologize to Stanfield. Since he didn't trust the public enough to apologize to it, Canadians didn't trust Trudeau.

Inflation was a symptom of a broad and fundamental problem in Canada. The country's long, postwar economic expansion was coming to an end. It was less and less competitive internationally. Instead of letting the free market system work on its own, the government was putting in place more rules. Trudeau mused about a "New Society" in which sharing and caring would replace competitiveness and greed. In one speech he commented: "We can't rely on the free market system any more. We need rules."

For a philosopher, these ideas would have been fine; for a Canadian political leader, they were destructive. When Canadians heard Trudeau's speculations about increasing control over the economy, they worried that he was beginning to sound like a socialist rather than a capitalist.

Canadians no longer trusted him as an economic leader. All that was left for him to do was to keep the public more or less quiet by postponing the paying of the country's bills. Year after year he announced budget deficits. Harsh measures to reduce the debt would have to wait for another prime minister.

Yes, many things had gone wrong for Trudeau between 1974 and 1976. In fact, in 1976, his approval rating in the polls was only 19 per cent, a ranking lower than any prime minister had received since polling began in Canada. Trudeau's descent had been complete and quick. Whatever comes up must come down—he had proved that. Was it equally true that whatever comes down must come up again?

Chapter 6
Two Voices, One Canada

For nine days in June 1976, there were no jet trails in Canadian skies. All airlines grounded their planes because of a strike by air traffic controllers, worried that a new policy of compulsory bilingualism might threaten their jobs. Pierre Trudeau went on national television to appeal for an end to the strike. Nothing happened. In the House of Commons, he called the strike "the worst crisis to national unity since the Conscription Crisis [of the First World War]." Nothing happened.

On the streets, people were buying T-shirts that showed a beaver (representing Canada) strangling a frog (representing Quebec), and western Canadian radio stations were airing an editorial that began with "Quebec, go suck a lemon" and ended with "I want a divorce. No fault. No contest."

Trudeau's dream of turning Canada into a bilingual country that could be, as he put it, "a brilliant prototype for the moulding of tomorrow's civilization" was turning into a nightmare.

One of the causes was the Act Respecting the Official Languages, which Trudeau had introduced into the Commons on October 17, 1968. He described it as "a conscious choice we are making about the future of Canada." Trudeau was committed to bilingualism for the country and to making francophones a full part of the federal government. He allowed nothing to stop him, neither increasing opposition in English Canada nor Quebec's sideways shift toward official unilingualism.

Bilingualism had been integral to Trudeau's version of federalism from his earliest days at *Cité Libre*. He saw it as an inherent right of francophones, one of Canada's two founding peoples. (It was not until years later that Native peoples would be recognized as a third founding people.) "Language is related to man's life in society as breathing is related to life itself," declared his bilingualism policy. Trudeau regarded any step backward from bilingualism not merely as cowardice or disloyalty but, more strongly, as heresy. Trudeau pointed out that francophones and anglophones were not treated equally in the civil service. For example, in the mid-1960s, francophones were 27 per cent of the national population but held only 10 per cent of all civil service posts. Trudeau believed that only equal treatment of francophones and anglophones in the civil service could make Ottawa a capital that truly represented the nation.

After bilingualism was legislated in 1968, thousands of English-speaking civil servants tried, many with no success, to learn enough French to qualify for promotion. Outside Ottawa, resistance to the Act grew as people across the country realized that bilingualism—very difficult to achieve in, say, B.C. or Newfoundland where there are few French speakers—effectively excluded them from civil service jobs. Trudeau's near-defeat in the 1972 election undoubtedly reflected in part this backlash against bilingualism.

In response, he moderated the policy, providing help to enable unilingual civil servants to learn the second language. A report by Official Languages Commissioner Keith Spicer released in March 1976 revealed the embarrassing discovery that only 11 per cent of anglophone civil servants reached fluency in French after their studies and 80 per cent of them scarcely ever used the language afterward. As an alternative to official bilingualism, Spicer recommended the so-called schools option, which would encourage the learning of French in the nation's schools so that all Canadians, not just civil servants, would come to have a stake in the program. Trudeau, however, worried that the schools option would take too long: "We can't tell Quebecers, 'Cool it, fellows, in 40 years we might be able to talk to you.'"

He had less time than he thought. In 1976, Premier Robert Bourassa enacted Bill 22, which made Quebec officially unilingual in French. This won Bourassa and the provincial Liberals some applause from Quebec nationalists; Trudeau and the federal

Liberals, however, received a chorus of boos from the rest of the country. When the air traffic controllers strike began that summer, prompted by concerns about how bilingualism would affect jobs, anglophone resentment against Bill 22 helped trigger public support for the strike. In response, imposing bilingualism upon the controllers became a rallying point for francophones. The "two solitudes," as Canadian author Hugh MacLennan had famously referred to the French and English in his 1945 novel of that title, were now dubbed the "two hostilities" by separatist leader René Lévesque.

Then, suddenly, the crisis over language became irrelevant. On November 15, 1976, before 15,000 ecstatic, delirious, disbelieving supporters in a Montreal downtown arena, René Lévesque came to the microphone to accept congratulations for the Parti Québécois's astonishing election victory. He said: "I never thought I would be so proud to be a Quebecer."

Journalist René Lévesque in Korea, 1951, during the Korean War

No two leaders could be less alike—or have more in common—than Trudeau and Lévesque. Trudeau—glamorous, sexy, brilliant, and worldly—was the person every Quebecer wanted to be. Lévesque—an incessant smoker wearing crumpled suits, passionate, compassionate, eloquent, and funny—was the person every Quebecer thought himself to be. A former broadcaster,

Lévesque become a politician and was a key member of the Quiet Revolution team of 1960.

Gradually, his views became separatist, yet he always maintained contact with English Canadians and never yielded to bigotry or extremism. To Lévesque, separatism was not so much separation from the rest of the country as an affirmation that Quebec was, and had to be, "this one corner of the earth where we can be completely ourselves … the only place where we can really be at home." He fought two elections and lost both. He heard Trudeau pronounce dismissively, "separatism is dead." Then came the incredible election result that caused even strong Quebec federalists to reveal, as publisher Roger Lemelin did, that "there were tears in my eyes and I didn't quite know why." Perhaps they were prompted by the pride and joy at a sense of oneness that many Quebecers felt that night and for weeks afterward.

Next to his near-defeat in the 1972 election, the election of the Parti Québécois was the greatest political crisis Trudeau had ever faced. Lévesque made a promise to have a province-wide referendum on separation, giving the people a direct vote on the issue. It seemed unlikely that he could lose it. Trudeau's public response to the idea of a referendum was one of cool, lethal calm; he showed neither alarm nor anger. He pointed out that Quebecers had exercised their democratic right to elect the government they wanted, but he was adamant that the new government's mandate did not extend automatically to separation. In a later televised speech, he promised "cooperation in every form" to the new government at Quebec City and ruled out force to keep the province in Confederation, but he said that for Quebec to separate from Canada would be "a sin against the spirit, a sin against humanity."

Trudeau denied Lévesque any target to aim at and so bought time for himself and for the country to regain equilibrium. And as time passed, change began. In February 1977, Trudeau was back on top of the national polls for the first time in years—with an approval rating of 51 per cent. Trudeau's marriage ended in May 1977, and when he became a single parent, Canadians found him appealing in this new role. They reconnected with their prime minister. Suddenly, he seemed human, vulnerable, alone, and facing the cares of a single parent. Also, Lévesque's very success in becoming premier of Quebec began to have the effect of scaring English Canadians. Worried that Quebec would separate from Canada, quite a few Quebecers turned back to Trudeau, seeing him as the one political champion who knew how to deal with this crisis of Confederation.

Across the country, members of the public confessed on radio shows and in letters to newspapers that they might have contributed to the election victory of the separatist party by criticizing bilingualism. Parents in every province were now pushing their children into French immersion courses and schools. Service clubs, churches, and voluntary organizations held seminars on national unity. No one wanted to hear any more complaints about bilingualism from the air traffic controllers.

Lévesque began to moderate his language. His goal, he said, was not to "destroy Canada" but to win a "new deal" for Quebec. To try to regain the initiative, he enacted Bill 101. This declared that English was no longer an official language in Quebec and could no longer be used by right in the provincial legislature. As well, on all signs, words in French had to be much larger than those in English. All firms in Quebec with more than 50 employees would have to qualify for "Francization" certificates to confirm that French was their principal language of use.

Trudeau denounced the legislation as "retrograde." Across the country, the public's response was muted, as if Canadians were reluctant to inflame the tensions that were already endangering national unity. (Later, criticism would mount against the so-called language police who imposed fines on firms and stores that had English words in almost the same size as French ones.) Instead people began to accept that Quebec would always be overwhelmingly French and the rest of the country (New Brunswick excepted) would naturally be essentially English. Bilingualism would be limited, but where it existed, such as the federal government and the upper levels of national organizations and associations, it would be everywhere. It wasn't a grand solution of the kind Trudeau once envisaged, but it was a workable compromise.

Chapter 7
Defeat

In politics, as in war, there is a "tipping point"; after this point, either success reinforces success or failure multiplies failure. Pierre Trudeau's tipping point happened in the fall of 1977. By then, most Canadians no longer feared that Quebecers might follow up their election of the Parti Québécois by actually voting for sovereignty-association in a referendum. This was a considerable triumph for Trudeau. But it meant that Canadians no longer needed him to keep the country together. Some of his aides urged him to call a snap election before his support ebbed too far. (Elections are usually held every four years.) Fearing it would have been too blatantly opportunist, Trudeau chose not to.

His government began to lose direction over the following months, but Prime Minister Trudeau himself still had allure and appeal. At a Liberal policy convention in Ottawa in February 1978, Trudeau vaulted to the stage, spread his feet apart, and stuck his thumbs into his belt in what became known as his "gunslinger" pose. Canadians also admired the courage with which Trudeau faced the stories that were spreading around Ottawa about his wife's inappropriate behaviour, the grace with which he handled his and Margaret's subsequent separation, and the care and devotion with which he brought up his three sons.

Trudeau with his sons at 24 Sussex Drive

But about his actual job of running the country, there was astonishingly little to be said. After two decades of the Liberals being continuously in power—since Lester Pearson had been prime minister—the party was tired and stale. The economy was running down. Canada was inexorably losing international competitiveness. The budget was permanently in deficit, with the national debt increasing by more than $30 billion a year. Taxes kept rising, as did government spending and the number of civil servants (a growth of 127 per cent between 1970 and 1976 when the population increased by just 8 per cent), meaning an extra burden on taxpayers to pay their salaries. In Britain, a new kind of economics—which involved tax cuts, deregulation, privatization, less dependence on government and more reliance on the marketplace—was being initiated by Prime Minister Margaret Thatcher. Similar economic strategies would soon be put in place in the United States by President Ronald Reagan.

In Ottawa, neither Trudeau nor anyone around him could think of what to do; doing something new would have meant admitting that much of what the Liberals had done in the past decade had been wrong or at best irrelevant. When, in mid-1978, Trudeau did make a change, announcing that government spending was to be cut by $2.5 billion to reduce the deficit, he surprised even his own finance minister, Jean Chrétien, who had not been told of the new policy. This huge and seemingly random cut had no discernible effect upon the size of the deficit. Instead, it only served to confirm the arguments of those, including the Conservatives and businessmen, who kept saying that Trudeau had lost control over government spending.

Trudeau was now isolated from most of his own ministers and members of Parliament. In 1977 he had begun spending all of his time with a small group of senior aides, including Michael Pitfield and Jim Coutts. In October of that year, he had called 15 by-elections on the same day and, in the worst drubbing ever suffered by a prime minister, lost all of them except a pair of seats in Quebec that had always voted Liberal. He got a political break in the spring of 1978 when Joe Clark, leader of the Progressive Conservative Party, made a round-the-world tour to raise his image but instead diminished it by losing his luggage. In March 1979, Trudeau made a sudden visit to Governor General Ed Schreyer, and then called a federal election for May 22, 1979.

The election's result was certain from the start. Clark, far ahead in the polls, complained from his home town of High River, Alberta, that Canada was "a community of communities," but otherwise said as little as possible. Trudeau spent much of his time name-calling: Clark was "a puppet of the premiers"; a farmer heckling him was "a professional complainer"; and Premiers Peter Lougheed of Alberta and Allan Blakeney of Saskatchewan, because they were fighting the federal government, were "enemies of Confederation."

Saskatchewan Premier Allan Blakeney

Only in the last few weeks of the election campaign, when defeat was certain, did Trudeau refind his true voice. At a mass rally in Toronto, he described how he would try to get the premiers to agree to a new constitution, including a bill of rights. (Our constitution was the 110-year-old British North America Act, which lacked a bill of rights, unlike in the U.S.) If that failed he would act on his own, but with the support of the people. He enthused: "We will have a Canadian constitution, made by Canadians for Canadians, and we will do it together." He got little applause. A day later, in Hamilton, Ontario, he proclaimed: "Either we will have one strong united country or we will have ten principalities. Let us bring it all together in one gigantic act of national will."

The leaders debate during the 1979 campaign: Ed Broadbent, Trudeau and Joe Clark

Canadians still didn't vote for him. Clark won, and at just 39, the Conservative leader was the youngest prime minister ever.

Yet Pierre Trudeau went out in style. He made his concession speech with a smile on his face, a rose in his lapel, and the kind of defiant line that his hero Cyrano de Bergerac would have made: "With all its sham, drudgery, and broken dreams, it's still a

Pierre Trudeau drives away from Government House, June 4, 1979, in his Mercedes sports car after resigning as prime minister

beautiful world." Although he was defeated, he hadn't been crushed. He actually won more of the national vote (40 per cent to 36 per cent) than Clark, and by holding on to 136 seats, he'd kept the Conservatives from winning a majority government. When Trudeau left office on June 4, 1979, he called on the governor general at Rideau Hall. For five years, he had been driven through Ottawa in the official Cadillac. On this day, he was driving his own silver-grey Mercedes. "I'm free," he told reporters, and then roared off down the driveway.

Chapter 8
Fall and Rise

Pierre Trudeau was brave in defeat, but soon afterward he fell into a depression. He had to cut his staff in half and move from 24 Sussex to the gloomy "loser's" residence at Stornoway, the official residence of the Opposition. He'd lost the prime minister's lakeside cottage at Harrington Lake where he'd so often swum and canoed and, in recent years, often enjoyed the companionship of an attractive woman. He had to carry his own bags through airports and spend his own money. He was frugal but, at the best of times, had no idea how to handle money. In Toronto he once took a $6 taxi ride, gave the driver a quarter tip, and then asked uncertainly, "Is it enough?" The driver, recognizing him, said nothing.

Mostly, Trudeau hid. He stayed away from Liberal caucus meetings of members of Parliament, never met the press, and issued few statements. His one useful political act was shaving off the thick beard that he'd grown on a summer canoeing trip after an aide insisted that it made him look like a wild man rather than an Opposition leader.

On Wednesday, November 21, 1980, he walked into the Liberal caucus to announce his resignation as party leader: "It's all over." As his MPs and senators applauded him, Trudeau came close to tears. He bought an historic house in Montreal, designed by the Art Deco architect Ernst Cormier. Meanwhile, the process of holding a Liberal leadership convention to replace Trudeau was put in motion.

Trudeau then settled down to read his "obituaries," the journalists' and academics' comments on his 12 years in power.

Except for Quebec commentators, who were relatively kind to one of their own, they were almost unanimously critical, even scornful. "History will not be lenient to Mr. Trudeau," said the *Ottawa Citizen* in an editorial. He "deprived us of a rising national confidence and feeling, and left us in considerable constitutional and economic disarray," wrote columnist Douglas Fisher in the *Toronto Sun.*

Ordinary Canadians thought quite differently. Letters, telegrams, and phone calls flooded Trudeau's office, expressing a deep sense of loss. "He did this one magnificent thing," wrote Robin Carlsen in a letter to the *Victoria Times.* "He created passion where there was dullness, elegance where there was drabness, spontaneity where there was artifice, mystique where there was ordinariness."

Lévesque announces the wording of the referendum question

Trudeau began to bounce back in the polls. One other harbinger of the future occurred. Early in December, Lévesque announced the wording of the referendum question. Quebec polls put support for the sovereignty-association option well in the lead. The threat to national unity created a job for Trudeau, the champion of a united Canada, but he was now on the sidelines.

The Clark government was perhaps the most unlucky in Canadian history. It was elected because Canadians were fed up and bored with Trudeau, and because ordinary people were hurting economically. The Clark government's response was to bring down a budget (by Finance Minister John Crosbie) that set out, for the first time, to seriously address the urgent issue of the budget deficit. But it turned out that what the Canadian people really wanted was Trudeau.

Here's how the drama unfolded. It began off-stage. Polls showed that if Trudeau were back as leader, he—and the

Pierre Elliott Trudeau

Liberal Party—would easily win an election. Liberal Party members loyal to Trudeau looked for a way to precipitate that election.

On Tuesday, December 11, 1980, John Crosbie brought down his budget. Included in it was an 18-cent-a-gallon gasoline excise tax to raise additional revenues to apply against the deficit. In the House of Commons, Trudeau loyalists, such as Allan MacEachen, proclaimed that this small increase would hurl Canada straight into a depression. They made the same argument in the Liberal caucus meetings, whipping up Liberal MPs into a fighting mood. Trudeau, who no longer attended these planning meetings, gave them no encouragement. Nevertheless, MacEachen, aided by Coutts and others, ensured that all Liberals would be in Ottawa for the budget vote.

Conservative Finance Minister John Crosbie

At this point, Trudeau's tone began to change. When MacEachen told him that the government was likely to be defeated and that he'd better decide what he was going to do, Trudeau answered enigmatically, "What does one do? One does one's duty, of course."

Clark knew nothing about this growing tide of opposition. Absent Conservative ministers and MPs weren't ordered back immediately. Trudeau had tried to placate the New Democrats when he was prime minister of a minority government. The Conservatives, however, made no attempt to ensure the support of the New Democrats or the small group of Creditiste MPs.

The vote on Crosbie's budget was held late in the evening of Thursday, December 11. At 10:21 p.m. the votes were counted. The results were 139 to 133, and Clark was defeated. A day later, he called on the governor general to announce an election.

Prime Minister Joe Clark

The Liberal caucus met again. This time, Trudeau was there. He insisted that he had not asked to return as leader, but should the caucus "overwhelmingly" demand that he return he would respond to the call of duty and lead them in the election. He then left without a backward glance. Trudeau loyalists argued that the only justification for defeating the government had been to create a chance for Trudeau to return as leader, and subsequently as prime minister. Although many MPs favoured one or the other of the potential alternate leaders, in the end, the caucus agreed to invite Trudeau to return.

Trudeau appeared to mull over his options, although it's likely that he'd made up his mind long before and was now only playing coy. On Tuesday, December 18, Trudeau strode into a press conference to announce: "It is my duty to accept the draft [of the party]."

The result of the 1980 election was never in doubt. The one way Trudeau might have lost was if he'd reminded Canadians of why they'd voted against him only six months earlier. On the advice of campaign manager Keith Davey, he ran a "low-bridging" campaign, reading deliberately boring speeches in a monotone. Only in the campaign's last two weeks, when victory was certain, did Trudeau allow himself to enjoy the speech making, switching to the topics he cared about—national unity and the constitution.

On February 8, 1980, Trudeau came back to Ottawa's Chateau Laurier Hotel. It was here that he'd faced the crowds after his defeat in 1979. On this night, he won 147 seats, a comfortable majority and his best performance since his first election. Sixty years of age, he bounded up to the platform like a young athlete, with, as always, a red rose in his lapel. "Welcome to the '80s," Trudeau said with a broad, boyish grin.

Pierre Trudeau won, and Canada won.

The 1980 election handed Trudeau more power than any prime minister of modern times had ever had. His party had a majority and so was unbeatable in the House of Commons. Trudeau was both experienced—now the most senior leader in all Western democracies—and, as the election result showed, unchallengeably popular among Canadians.

There was almost no opposition to Trudeau now. Conservative leader Joe Clark was soon replaced by Brian Mulroney. The provincial premiers could still take pot shots at the prime minister, but only from a distance. Within the government, all his ministers, quite a few of whom had favoured other candidates for leader, were now cowed by Trudeau. He moved loyalists, such as Marc Lalonde, Allan MacEachen, Jean Chrétien, and Don Johnstone, into senior portfolios and brought back all his close aides, such as Michael Pitfield, Jim Coutts, and Michael Kirby.

Even his stormy relations with Margaret had mellowed. They quarrelled less and less over the upbringing of Sacha, Justin, and Michel. Also, Margaret was closer to her sons now, having moved to Ottawa.

Trudeau was as active, athletic, and energetic as ever. He had many girlfriends, such as the classical guitarist Leona Boyd, to keep him company. He could do just about anything he wanted.

After being sworn in as Canada's sixteenth prime minister, Trudeau shuffled his Cabinet, made some changes at the top of the civil service, and then called Parliament back into session just two months later. The Throne Speech promised activist government.

Conservative leader Brian Mulroney

The setting of the national agenda for the next five weeks was out of his hands, however. On April 15, the Quebec premier returned refreshed from a holiday in Bermuda to announce that May 20 would be an "historic day" in Quebec, the day that the province's citizens would vote in a referendum. Lévesque urged them to vote "Yes" to a convoluted question that essentially gave the government the right to negotiate sovereignty-association with the rest of the country.

The political odds favoured Lévesque. Polls put the "Yes" vote ahead at 47 per cent to 44 per cent. During the campaign, Lévesque's passionate speaking style and enormous personal appeal gave him the advantage over the dry intellectualism of the leader of the "No" forces, Claude Ryan, Quebec Liberal leader and former editor of the Quebec City-based daily newspaper, *Le Devoir*. In the weeks leading up to the referendum,

Lévesque cagily avoided all references to separatism or even to sovereignty-association. He said only that a "Yes" vote would give Quebecers a chance to win "equality as a people"; any actual constitutional change, such as a move toward sovereignty-association, would be effected only if approved in a second referendum.

Many federalists in Quebec, as well as in Ottawa, urged Trudeau not to take part in the referendum debate. They believed that defeat was likely for those on the side of federalism, and that it would be better for Trudeau to preserve his credibility for the actual negotiations about sovereignty-association, which would come later.

No one who knew him doubted for a second that Trudeau would do anything but charge directly into the battle wherever it was fiercest. Showing his new canniness, he initially let Jean Chrétien, a Quebecer himself, lead the fight for him from Ottawa. Chrétien engaged in appealing rhetoric. "Why should Quebecers separate?" he asked. "To make us lose our Canadian passports? To make us lose the riches that have always belonged to us?"

Trudeau with Jean Chrétien and René Lévesque

Pierre Elliott Trudeau

Holding himself back, Trudeau spoke in the Commons right after Lévesque announced the referendum date, but he used dry, technical language. Trudeau pointed out that even if Lévesque did win a mandate from the people of Quebec to negotiate sovereignty-association, the federal government had no constitutional right to negotiate this. A "Yes" vote would only result in constitutional deadlock. Trudeau stayed above the fray, and by doing so, he built up excitement about what he would do when he did enter it.

What he did was to come in sideways. First, Trudeau attacked the idea that separatists were somehow more honourable and idealistic than federalists. He pointed out that the separatists had put to Quebecers "a conditional and ambiguous question." Where was the honour in that? Then he attacked their pride. "It takes more courage to stay in Canada than to retreat behind our walls," he said in Quebec City.

In politics, luck is the most priceless asset of all. Earlier, the Péquistes (supporters of the Parti Québécois) had made a crashing mistake when one of their leaders, Lise Payette, made a dismissive reference to Claude Ryan's wife as an "Yvette," which is derogatory slang for a silent, docile housewife. Federalists seized on the comment; they formed Yvette clubs of Quebec federalist women, many of them feminists and successful professionals, who denounced the sexism of their opponents.

Then Lévesque made an even more crashing mistake. Sensing that the tide was turning against him, he lashed out at his old rival and tormentor, Trudeau. It was natural for Pierre Elliott Trudeau not to be in favour of separation, declared Lévesque, "because his middle name is English."

Trudeau strode into the heart of the battle. On May 15 he staged a huge rally at Montreal's Paul Sauvé Arena, the same one where four years earlier Lévesque had accepted cascades of applause for the stunning election victory of the Parti Québécois. The crowd chanted out the familiar war cry, "Tru-deau, Tru-deau, Tru-deau," and a new cry, "Ell-i-ott, Ell-i-ott, Ell-i-ott." Trudeau challenged Lévesque directly. He agreed that his middle name was Elliott: "It was borne by the Elliotts who came to

Canada two hundred years ago." He went on, "My name is a
Quebec name, and it is also a Canadian name." He then cited the
duality of many of Lévesque's ministers—Daniel Johnson, Robert
Burns, Louis O'Neill. "This is the kind of division we are saying
'no' to."

It was epic oratory. And what followed was brilliant politics.
A "No" vote, said Trudeau, wouldn't be a "No" to change. He
made a "solemn declaration" that a "No" vote, or separatism's
defeat, would be "a mandate to change the constitution, to renew
federalism."

On May 20, Trudeau won, and Canada won—decisively.
The results reflected 60 per cent for federalism and 40 per cent
for separatism. Not only had a majority of Quebecers voted for
federalism, but a majority of francophone Quebecers had, as
well. Within a few months, Marcel Pepin, editor of the newspaper *Le Soleil*, wrote: "It's over. Not only separatism, but
nationalism as well."

The referendum had deeply divided Quebecers, setting
friends against each other and splitting families. People now
turned away from politics and toward economics and business.
Even when Lévesque won re-election the next year, there was no
upset in the rest of the country nor any rekindling of nationalism
within Quebec.

But Trudeau had one more national unity challenge to meet.
This one came from one of the newest parts of Canada, Alberta.

Chapter 9
A New Canada

Much of the time, leaders don't really lead. They spend most of their time in power reacting to events over which they have little or no control. Occasionally, however, those in power have a chance to rewrite history. Pierre Trudeau's moment of opportunity occurred in 1980–81 after the victory in the referendum.

It was only a sliver of an opportunity, caused by a combination of two things: English Canada's relief and gratitude for Trudeau's having "saved" Canada, and Quebecers' search for something to recover from the wreckage of all their lost hopes for nationalism and separatism. The public's receptive mood wouldn't last long because other events would wear away at it. Trudeau recognized this. At the risk of almost tearing the country apart, he used it to rewrite Canadian history more decisively than any leader since John A. Macdonald, who had successfully brought Canada into Confederation and become the new country's first prime minister.

The day after the referendum vote, Trudeau rose in the House of Commons. He announced that he would move immediately to fulfill the pledge he'd made to Quebecers that federalism would be renewed and the constitution patriated from Britain. (Canada had once been a British colony and subject to British laws. Canada's constitution still could only be legally amended by Britain. Trudeau wanted to patriate the constitution, which meant transferring the legal power to amend Canada's constitution from Britain to Ottawa.) That same night, Jean Chrétien left Ottawa and began visiting all the premiers—except

Lévesque, who refused to see him—to discuss Trudeau's plans with them.

In one way or another, Trudeau had thought about the constitution all his adult life. Many even accused him of being obsessive about it. As prime minister, though, he denied this. "I am not in a frantic hurry to change the constitution," he told *Maclean's* magazine in 1974, "because I am in a frantic hurry to change reality." (By this he meant that he wanted to change Canada's reality by initiating political reform, administrative change, efficiency in government.)

He became increasingly focused on the constitution because Quebec governments, federalist and separatist, focused so much on it. The constitution outlined the balance of power between the federal government and the provincial governments, and this is what Quebec was challenging.

Robert Bourassa

Wresting jurisdiction and power from the federal government became almost an obsession at Quebec City, the seat of the Quebec provincial government. And as the years passed, other premiers would want an equal share of the spoils.

In his first term as prime minister (1968–72), Trudeau had come agonizingly close to achieving patriation of the constitution. In June 1971, he and the premiers had met at Victoria, B.C., and to their own great surprise and delight had agreed on a modest constitutional package of patriation, a limited bill of rights, and the handing over to the provinces of the right to nominate Supreme Court judges. But Quebec nationalists put fierce pressure on Robert Bourassa, the youthful Quebec premier, as soon as he returned home from the meeting, and Bourassa had withdrawn his approval. Moreover, he henceforth put increasing distance between himself and his fellow Liberals in Ottawa. Bourassa started talking about "profitable federalism," as if only money justified Quebecers staying in Canada, and about "cultural sovereignty."

The western provinces had growing economic power and wealth and increasing self-confidence. To complicate constitutional matters, these oil-rich provinces, which despised the Liberals' national energy policy with its subsidized oil prices, began to act almost as aggressively as Quebec in demanding jurisdiction and power. Conservative leader Joe Clark took the side of the provinces. In response, Trudeau dismissed Clark as "a head-waiter to the premiers" and declared that Canada had to amount to "more than a collection of shopping centres."

It would be an exaggeration to say that for the past half-decade the premiers, as leaders of the provinces, had run Canada. But a number of them, most especially Quebec's René Lévesque, Alberta's Peter Lougheed, and Newfoundland's Brian Peckford, had evolved a notion of Confederation as a compact between the provinces with Ottawa as a kind of coordinating secretariat. As well, areas over which the provinces had jurisdiction, such as health and education, were constantly expanding, while those areas over which Ottawa had jurisdiction, such as defence, were contracting. In the late 1970s, the premiers had kept Trudeau on the defensive. At one time, after granting the provinces a series of concessions, he admitted, "Maybe I've given away the shop myself."

Now Trudeau had to come up with a way to get all the premiers to agree with his constitutional proposals. His tactic was to out-flank them. He divided his constitutional proposals into two groups. One, for Trudeau by far the most important, was the "people's package." It consisted of the bill of rights and the patriation of the constitution. The other was the "government package," which was comprised of all the jurisdictional concessions the provinces wanted in return for agreeing to the "people's package." The premiers were dismayed. It appeared that their demands were being placed second, and Trudeau had set up the "packages" so that the public was being lined up against them. Trudeau increased the pressure on the provinces to come to an agreement by disclosing, at a First Ministers' conference in Ottawa in June 1980, that if agreement wasn't reached, he would go to London unilaterally, acting for the federal government alone, and ask for the constitution to be patriated with a bill of rights added to it. He would get his "people's package" without the approval of the provinces.

A second conference that September left the premiers even angrier. Trudeau said that, if there was no provincial agreement, he would get a constitutional resolution passed by the Commons and Senate, both of which he controlled, and go with this to London.

One of those fortunate accidents by which great events are decided occurred at this point. The Conservatives were deliberately delaying the passage of Trudeau's constitutional resolution in the Commons. Although he feared it would cause further delays, Trudeau agreed to allow the resolution to be considered by a joint Commons-Senate Committee. He also agreed that these sessions could be televised. There was an unexpected result. For the first time, the public began to learn about the bill of rights, which became known as the Charter of Rights and Freedoms. The more English Canadians learned about it, the more they liked it. They especially liked seeing that many proposals for changes to the Charter, most particularly by women's groups and those representing the disabled, were accepted by the committee, making the Charter truly a people's document. This public support for the Charter never wavered through all the political struggles ahead.

The premiers counter-attacked. Eight of them formed what became known as the "Gang of Eight." (Bill Davis of Ontario and Richard Hatfield of New Brunswick, both of them unflinching Trudeau allies, stayed out of the "gang.") They initiated legal challenges to the federal government's right to act unilaterally. They tried to whip up opposition among backbench MPs in London and muster up some British allies, even though Prime Minister Margaret Thatcher had from the start committed herself to passing the legislation. A British Commons committee gave the premiers a partial victory by recommending that "substantial" provincial agreement was needed before London should approve Trudeau's legislation.

By the spring of 1981, the first of the provincial premiers' three court challenges had been decided by a provincial supreme court, the Newfoundland Supreme Court. It decreed that unilateral constitutional change by Trudeau would be illegal. Although the courts in Manitoba and Quebec later ruled in his favour, Trudeau, to break the deadlock, referred the issue to the highest appeal court of Canada, the Supreme Court in Ottawa. The Supreme Court's ruling, which came late in September 1981, was a classic Canadian compromise. By a margin of six judges to three, the court decreed that the premiers' claim that "substantial" provincial approval was needed for constitutional change was valid. But by a vote of seven to two, the judges ruled that Trudeau had the legal right, although not necessarily the political right, to unilaterally ask London to approve his package.

Trudeau with Britain's prime minister, Margaret Thatcher

Trudeau's response was deft. He would press on, he said, but he would make one last attempt to win provincial agreement at a First Ministers' conference. It would be held in Ottawa in the renovated railway station just outside the Chateau Laurier Hotel in the first week of November 1981.

From the rap of the gavel that opened the November 1981 conference with the ten premiers in Ottawa, Pierre Trudeau dominated the process. It was as if the leader knew that his encounter with destiny had arrived and he was ready for it. Trudeau was cool, soft-voiced, controlled, but also menacing and intimidating. Ontario's Bill Davis and New Brunswick's Richard Hatfield remained his single allies. Among the eight dissident premiers, all but Lévesque were uneasily aware of the critical fact that their constituents were overwhelmingly in support of the Charter and patriation of the constitution. Trudeau let them stew in the uncertainty. He said little on the conference's first two days, then casually tossed out the idea of having a national referendum if agreement were impossible.

Ontario Premier Bill Davis

All of the anglophone premiers were deeply worried by the referendum idea: most expected they would lose a vote in their own province. Even the one or two premiers who might "win" a majority of "no" votes knew that the referendum would bitterly divide the country. Lévesque was the least worried about having a referendum because Quebecers were strongly opposed to Trudeau's unilateralism.

Lévesque's position seemed strong but Trudeau spotted its weakness. He targeted Lévesque as the group's weakest link. He taunted Lévesque, saying, "You're the great believer in referendums. You can't be opposed to one … Or are you afraid to take me on?" Lévesque responded by rising to the bait: "Okay, I'd like to fight the Charter," he said. For the first time, Lévesque had taken a position different from that of his "Gang of Eight" allies, who did not want a referendum. Like a matador, Trudeau had goaded the bull into running onto his sword. Initially only Trudeau appreciated what had happened, but he gave no sign of this. He instantly adjourned the conference for lunch, and went straight to the press microphones to comment sarcastically on the "new Quebec-Canada alliance." But asked by reporters what was going on, he replied with a gleam in his eyes, "The cat is among the pigeons."

After lunch, now appreciating the mistake he'd made, Lévesque raised objections to possible federal rules on a potential referendum. It was all too late. After the meetings ended, others among the Eight began to seek out federal officials and ministers, looking for some kind of a compromise to avoid a national referendum that could be so embarrassing to them.

The most important private meeting resulted in a so-called kitchen accord between Jean Chrétien and Saskatchewan Attorney-General Roy Romanow; they hammered out a deal including a so-called notwithstanding clause, which would allow the premiers, in quite limited circumstances, to exempt themselves from the Charter of Rights in instances where local, provincial concerns were judged more important than the actual rights specified in the Charter. Trudeau remained adamantly opposed to a notwithstanding clause, which would weaken the civil rights that he had sought to enshrine in his new constitution.

René Lévesque, Allan MacEachen (left), and Richard Hatfield at the First Ministers' conference

Back at 24 Sussex Drive that evening, Trudeau argued the pros and cons of a compromise deal with his senior ministers and aides. While this was going on, nine of the premiers (all but Lévesque) and their aides were visiting one another's hotel rooms to informally haggle over clauses and paragraphs in the proposed Charter. Lévesque was conspicuous by his absence, politically, because he was not on board with the common goal and, physically, because he alone was staying in a hotel across the river in Hull, Quebec. In the end Trudeau's ministers persuaded him to agree to add the notwithstanding clause to the Charter. Later he would say he had done this "to my everlasting regret." The evening session, resulting in the anglophone premiers making a deal with the federal government while no Quebecers were present, became known in Quebec as the

"Night of the Long Knives," as an expression of their feeling of betrayal.

At the conference the next day, Lévesque glowered but said little as the premiers and Trudeau went through the details of the deal they had struck—patriation of the constitution and the Charter of Rights and Freedoms, but qualified by a notwith-standing clause. There were a few last-minute changes, like a commitment to a First Ministers' conference on Aboriginal issues. Except for the addition of the notwithstanding clause to the Charter of Rights, Trudeau had essentially won everything he had aimed for when he began the constitutional process over a year earlier. He had won everything he had aimed for all his life in terms of renewed federalism and a revised constitution.

Trudeau and Queen Elizabeth signing the constitution in Ottawa, 1982

Approval in London was now a formality. In April 1982, Queen Elizabeth came to Ottawa. In reality, Canada had been

Pierre Elliott Trudeau

an independent nation state for a long time. That spring, the Queen presided over the ceremony by which the country *legally* became a fully independent nation state.

Trudeau had realized a lifelong dream. He'd made the constitution wholly Canadian. It could now be altered in Canada without requiring London's approval. More important, it contained the Charter of Rights and Freedoms, the most liberal charter of any in the world. Incorporated into the constitution were all the linguistic rights that Trudeau had pursued for so long, such as the so-called mobility rights, which ensured that students, anglophone or francophone, moving to a different province could continue to be taught in their language of study. Lastly, the constitution contained a guarantee of equalization payments to the poorer provinces.

Lévesque refused to sign the document. He denounced it, claiming that the anglophone premiers and the federal government had ganged up on Quebec. Trudeau retorted that all of the signatures on the constitution, except the Queen's, had been those of francophones (Trudeau, Chrétien, and Solicitor-General André Ouellet) and it had been approved by all the Quebec MPs and senators. Nevertheless, the hard fact remained that Quebec had been excluded from the rewriting of the constitution of the country of which its people were one of the two founding peoples. There was unfinished business here that would have to be addressed, even though it might be by somebody else at some other time.

By the time the new constitution was in place, Trudeau was halfway through his mandate. Now his job as prime minister became that of an economic manager—or, more accurately, a manager of economic decline.

Chapter 10

Go West, Old Man

During the 1970s and 1980s Canada went through a period of economic decline. This could be measured most easily by the size of the country's annual budget deficit—which meant that to maintain our standard of living we had to spend money that we didn't have. Year in, year out, the deficit ran to about $30 billion. Every year's shortfall added to the national debt. Every year, this ate into a larger and larger share of the money that the government was able to raise with taxes, eventually gobbling up one-third of the government's total tax revenues. The result was that less money was available to be spent on government programs and policies.

The public became more and more resistant to paying taxes. Increasingly, the public's mood was cynical.

The reasons for the economic decline in Canada were debated endlessly. The most obvious cause was the impact of the steep increase in oil prices engineered by the international Organization of Petroleum Exporting Countries (OPEC) in the 1970s. (At its peak, there was a tenfold increase in prices.) Because the Canadian government had to pay more for oil and gas, there was less money available to spend on other things.

There was also more and more finger-pointing at economic policy itself as a cause for the decline. Since the end of World War II, the government had "fine-tuned" the economy, sometimes pumping in more money to force-feed economic growth, sometimes cutting back the money supply to choke off inflation. Britain's Prime Minister Thatcher and, from 1982 on, American

President Ronald Reagan were showing that a radically different economic policy could be an alternative. Dubbed neo-conservatism, this philosophy put faith in the marketplace and sought less reliance on government interference in the market. It called for government itself to be reduced by deregulation, by privatization (of government agencies), and by spending cuts. At the same time, government would reduce taxes and thereby provide incentives for entrepreneurs to create more wealth.

There was increasing public debate in Canada about the option of neo-conservative economics. For Canadians, it seemed to pose a double challenge. Cutting back on Canada's social programs, such as the healthcare system, would reduce the country's national distinctiveness. As well, relying on the marketplace would mean relying more and more on American corporations, which dominated the North American market. With fewer rules to control their activities in Canada, these American corporations might buy up the newly privatized Crown corporations, thus further reducing Canada's control over its own economy.

For Trudeau, this style of hands-off economics posed a particular personal challenge. It contradicted the policies he had been implementing ever since he'd come to office.

From his earliest days in office, Trudeau had had difficulties with western Canada. There was strong opposition to his bilingualism policy there. Many westerners saw bilingualism as a way of keeping them away from the centre of the country since they themselves had few opportunities to become bilingual. Western sensibilities were rubbed raw when pro-bilingualism commentators from central Canada referred to them as "rednecks." An early federal decree that the "RCMP" that appeared on officers' cars should be changed to the bilingual *Police* angered westerners since the Mounties had played a key role in the opening up of the West. (The decree was hastily rescinded.)

The root problem of Trudeau's difficulties was pretty straightforward. He knew nothing about the West and, during his early terms, he was in no mood to learn. At that time, his focus was on Quebec and only secondarily on the rest of the country. As prime minister he seldom went to the western provinces. (He did occasionally visit Vancouver, where he had several friends and where Margaret lived before they were married. The consequences of the few trips he did make were almost uniformly disastrous. At one time, he challenged prairie farmers with the unsympathetic question, "Why should I sell your wheat?")

Trudeau never understood why western Canada calls itself by the proud, visionary boast "Tomorrow Country." The first westerners had added their territory to Confederation by breaking the hard land, living in sod huts, and struggling to survive the brutal winters. He never understood that westerners felt themselves to be special, just as Quebecers did.

No Canadian leader can be popular everywhere, and this alienation between the prime minister and one of the country's four regions might not have mattered greatly—except that by the mid-1970s the West was beginning to command, and to demand, more attention. For one thing, the West was becoming wealthier.

Alberta was an oil-rich province, and when oil prices began to rise in the early 1970s, it brought incredible revenues to the province. But, although this was certainly a major factor in the region's elevated status, it was by no means the only one.

In the western provinces, and especially in Alberta, there was a booming self-confidence and entrepreneurial spirit. Cities like Edmonton and Calgary began to mature into cosmopolitan centres. The region developed political champions, such as Peter Lougheed, Alberta's premier, and Allan Blakeney, Saskatchewan's premier, who chafed under Ottawa's paternalism. They were determined to follow Quebec's lead and make

Alberta Premier Peter Lougheed

their provinces into thriving societies, and they wanted to do this by using their own resources instead of depending on hand-me-downs from the national capital.

In 1973, the revenues of the Alberta government began to soar as world oil prices rose. Lougheed and Trudeau quarrelled fiercely over the division of the take of the windfall revenues. Eventually, they agreed that the province would receive 45 per cent, the oil industry would receive 45 per cent, and 10 per cent would be allocated to the federal government. This share, on behalf of all Canadians, was distinctly small. Trudeau's achievement, his first energy policy, was to perpetuate the national policy of cheap oil for Canadians. (The price of oil to consumers was artificially set by the federal government; Canadians paid only half the actual world price.) By 1980, oil prices in Canada were so low that Americans were driving across the border just to fill up their gas tanks. Trudeau's policy ended up as a massive subsidy that encouraged over-consumption at a time when Canadian oil supplies were dwindling.

Back in power in 1980, Trudeau set out to correct his mistakes of the past and to secure a larger share of oil profits to the benefit of all Canadians. He appointed his best and toughest minister, Marc Lalonde, as minister of energy. In an election campaign during which he had said little of importance, Trudeau had given one meaningful speech (which he had allowed Lalonde to write for him) calling

Marc Lalonde

for a made-in-Canada energy policy. On October 28, 1980, Lalonde introduced his National Energy Policy (NEP). This was perhaps the most ambitious attempt at economic interventionism in Canada since Prime Minister John A. Macdonald's National Policy. One of the goals of the NEP was that 50 per cent of the U.S.-dominated oil and gas industry in Canada would be Canadian-owned by 1990, thus giving Canada full control over its own resources. Ottawa would take over "several large (foreign) oil companies." Ottawa's share of the revenue generated from oil would increase from 10 per cent to 23 per cent. To obtain this, Ottawa would impose a new tax on gas production, which meant the money would come mainly out of the pockets of the oil companies, leaving less revenue for Alberta.

Lougheed denounced the program as an attempt "to come into Alberta's living room." He objected both to Ottawa's taking a larger share of the revenues and to its intervening directly in the oil industry. To show that he was serious about his complaints, the premier cut back oil output in the province and withheld permits for two oil sands projects, deliberately jeopardizing Lalonde's attempt to reach his target of "self-sufficiency" by 1990. In Alberta, separatists suddenly appeared, some of them wearing T-shirts that said *Vive Alberta Libre* (Long Live a Free Alberta). Late in 1980, Trudeau told an aide, "I saved Quebec. Someone else will have to save the West."

The NEP actually had far less of an effect than Lalonde and Trudeau had anticipated. There were indeed a series of takeovers of U.S. oil companies by Canadian-owned Dome Petroleum and by the Crown corporation PetroCanada. But the NEP had been based on a simple, obvious error. It assumed that oil prices would continue rising, perhaps eventually to $100 a barrel. In fact, by the winter of 1980–81, a worldwide recession, and therefore a decrease in demand, caused oil prices to start dropping. This shaved away at the extra revenues Ottawa had counted on.

After implementing his energy policy, Trudeau simply held the line on the economic front. Substantial policy change would not occur in Canada until the late 1980s when Brian Mulroney, the Conservative prime minister, negotiated a Canada–U.S. free trade agreement.

Trudeau had just one more burst of creativity left. He had done all he could within Canada. Now he would venture outside it.

Chapter 11
Citizen of the World

Except for Lester Pearson, a former diplomat, no prime minister had come to office better informed about the world than Pierre Trudeau. He had travelled widely. He was multilingual, speaking English, French, and Spanish. He was completely at ease in all international capitals, except one: he was never entirely comfortable in Washington, the American capital. In fact, Trudeau seldom visited the U.S. and was uninterested in American politics, which was most unusual for a Canadian politician. Trudeau's terms as prime minister overlapped with the terms of three American presidents; although he got on exceptionally well with Jimmy Carter, his relations with Richard Nixon and Ronald Reagan were cool and distant.

Trudeau paid only intermittent attention to foreign affairs during the greater part of his first term. He did initiate an early White Paper, or official report, on foreign policy that rejected Canada's distinctive role as "helpful fixer," a role that Lester Pearson had supported. The White Paper proclaimed a new doctrine of "national interest," making Canada's own interests the focus of our foreign policy. Critics, including Lester Pearson himself, savaged the report. They pointed out that, by altering Canada's role as helpful fixer, it was altering an important part of Canada's identity. The criticism stung Trudeau and he soon dropped the phrase "national self-interest."

Without admitting he had been wrong to seek the change, Trudeau began to embrace "Pearsonianism," the idea of using foreign policy to project Canadian values abroad. In a 1974 speech at Duke University in Durham, North Carolina, Trudeau declared, "If I were to identify any single criterion by which I hope Canada's presence in the world would be judged, it would be by its humanitarianism." A year later, in a much-praised speech at London's Mansion House, he proclaimed the doctrine of "global sharing." He talked about sharing, and he acted on his words. Trudeau increased the budget of Canada's foreign aid program annually, and he initiated Canada World Youth, a program that arranged exchanges between young people from Canada and Third World countries. He also undertook some ambitious foreign policy initiatives such as extending diplomatic recognition to China in 1970 (Canada was the second western country after France to do so) and in 1969 to the Vatican. In subsequent years, he promoted the dialogue between northern and southern countries, co-chairing a major conference of rich and poor countries at Cancun, Mexico. Throughout all his terms in office, Trudeau maintained close and friendly relations with the president of communist Cuba, Fidel Castro. This irritated many politicians in Washington who made muted suggestions that Trudeau was a "communist," but it demonstrated Canada's commitment to helping poorer countries.

Trudeau's last major foreign policy initiative was his so-called peace initiative. The peace that Trudeau sought was in the Cold War rivalry between the U.S. and the Soviet Union. By the early 1980s, President Reagan was calling the Soviet Union an "evil empire." On September 1, 1983, the Soviets shot down a South Korean airliner that had wandered accidentally into their air space. Reagan denounced the Soviets for cold-blooded murder, ignoring his American intelligence reports that indicated otherwise. The situation quickly grew into a threatening international crisis.

Trudeau decided to try to lessen the overheated rhetoric of the two super-powers. On October 27, 1983, he announced his peace initiative in a speech at Guelph, Ontario; he would try to implement "a strategy of political confidence-building" between the two Cold War opponents.

In practical terms, no Canadian leader possessed the power to bring East and West together. Trudeau hoped at the very least to be able to cool the angry Washington–Moscow rhetoric. He set off on his mission, first touring the European capitals, from Brussels to The Hague to Paris to Bonn, in order to try and mobilize allies for his cause. His most important meeting was in London with British Prime Minister Margaret Thatcher, Reagan's close ally and a supporter of his strong tactics. Trudeau and Thatcher argued in private and in public about the need for a hard or soft position toward Moscow. He then flew to Tokyo, and then on to the Indian subcontinent for a meeting of the Commonwealth countries. He extracted from them a generalized statement of support for his soft approach. Much more effectively, and dramatically, he secured an invitation to visit Beijing.

By now Trudeau had talked to every leader who could influence an international peace accord except the two most crucial leaders, Reagan and Yuri Andropov, the Soviet secretary-general. In mid-December, Trudeau finally got his long-sought meeting with Reagan. On the advice of Canada's ambassador to Washington, Allan Gotlieb, Trudeau set out not to argue with Reagan, but to try to seduce him with flattery.

"I know you are a man of peace. And I know you are a great communicator," Trudeau told the aging president. Trudeau

Trudeau meets U.S. President Ronald Reagan

argued that Reagan was weakening his credentials as a man of peace with the language he was using. If Reagan "modified the rhetoric," he would be known as "a man of great power who was also a man of peace." Thereafter, whether by coincidence or as a result of his meeting with Trudeau, Reagan did tone down his language and never again used the phrase "evil empire."

Later, Trudeau went to Moscow to meet briefly with the new Soviet secretary-general, Yuri Andropov, at the funeral of his predecessor, but their meeting produced no results. But the modifying of Reagan's inflammatory language was the single clear accomplishment of Trudeau's peace initiative.

Trudeau had taken a public role in the highest levels of international affairs, something that no Canadian prime minister before him had dared to attempt. He thus brought foreign affairs home to Canadians. Canadians were proud to have such a leader, one with style, intelligence, and sophistication. Former U.S. Democratic vice-presidential nominee Walter Mondale praised him as "a priceless asset of the industrialized world." Joseph Kraft, a leading American columnist, described him as "perhaps the world's most gifted leader."

Trudeau's creed of "global sharing" became part of the Canadian consciousness. It led to Canadian initiatives such as the global ban on landmines and the international criminal court. In 2003 the United Nations, an international organization of countries set up to promote international peace and security, withheld its approval of the U.S. invasion of Iraq. As a result, Canadian Prime Minister Jean Chrétien refused to support the war, thus following in the tradition of Trudeau's foreign policy legacy and, before him, that of Lester Pearson.

It was now 1984 and Pierre Trudeau had been in office for an exceptionally long time. In all western democracies during the 50 years since World War II, only four leaders had been in power longer. (These were Tag Erlander of Sweden, Einar Gerhardsen of Norway, Jawaharlal Nehru of India, and Robert Menzies of Australia.) It was time for Trudeau to make up his mind whether to stay on for a while longer—or to leave.

Chapter 12
Political Afterlife and Death

Pierre Trudeau was now 64 years old. He had no remaining political agenda. Trudeau's main interest was guiding his three sons into their teenage years. His aides tried to convince Trudeau that he had to remain to fight on for liberalism, which was now increasingly threatened by a rising trend in neo-conservatism. Iona Campagnolo, Liberal Party president and a former Cabinet minister, was of a different mind, however. She told Trudeau that most party members believed that he had outstayed his time. She suggested that it was better for him to leave undefeated rather than go down in the crushing defeat that all the polls indicated lay ahead.

Iona Campagnolo

On the evening of February 27, 1984, Trudeau took a long walk in a blizzard that was raging through Ottawa. When he returned, his mind was made up. The next morning, he spoke to Iona Campagnolo by telephone and then called in his aides. Many responded with tears when he told them that he had decided not to remain as leader. Trudeau went home for lunch.

John Turner took over from Trudeau as the new Liberal leader. The former prime minister had left behind a vast number of patronage appointments that would place Trudeau's friends and supporters in public service offices as a "thank you" for their loyalty. Feeling he should carry through with Trudeau's promises, Turner went ahead and approved these appointments. He later regretted the decision. In the summer election, Conservative leader Brian Mulroney used this proof of political favouritism to go on to win the election with a huge majority.

Trudeau's last formal political act had taken place at the Ottawa Convention Centre in June 1984. Trudeau stood before his supporters one final time. On a giant screen was projected a film montage of Trudeau's years that covered footage of his sterling performance at the Jean Baptiste Day riot in Montreal during the 1968 election to highlights of his idealistic 1983–84 peace initiative. Then Trudeau came alone to the centre of the stage to deliver his creed for one last time. "Our hopes are high. Our faith in the people is great. Our courage is strong and our dreams for this beautiful country will never die." Trudeau's children, Justin, Sacha, and Michel, came out and the family held hands. Balloons went up, confetti rained down, and delegates roared out their love for their now lost hero.

Then Trudeau disappeared. He gave no press interviews. He made no comments about political affairs. He moved to Montreal into the historic Art Deco house that he'd purchased. He concentrated on educating, nurturing, and challenging his sons. He travelled often—to India's Himalayas, to the South Seas for scuba diving, to the Far East. He went on northern canoe trips with a small group of old friends. As far as anyone knew, he took no interest in Canadian current events, either under John Turner's brief leadership or Brian Mulroney's.

Prime Minister Brian Mulroney

Then, suddenly, he was back. Trudeau jumped onto the centre of the stage as magnetic, as brilliant, as ruthless as ever.

As anyone who knew him could have predicted, Trudeau was propelled back by a direct challenge. The instrument of his political resurrection was the Conservative prime minister, Brian Mulroney. Mulroney had come to power under the most difficult of circumstances. He followed on the heels of Trudeau and was therefore condemned to being constantly compared to him.

On April 29, 1987, at Meech Lake, north of Ottawa, the ten premiers gathered with Mulroney to talk over a series of constitutional changes. They had been discussing these issues over the last couple of years with no great sense of urgency. On a chilly, overcast day, they again went over familiar material that included declaring Quebec to be a "distinct society."

As the day wore on, the talks continued. Evening came, and arrangements were made to bring in a light dinner. By ten o'clock that night, the discussions were over. To their own astonishment, the ten premiers and the prime minister had agreed on a complete package that would enable Quebec (led once more by Bourassa) to sign on to the constitutional deal that Trudeau had wrangled out of the nine anglophone premiers and imposed upon an unwilling Quebec five years earlier. Canada's new constitution thus would for the first time gain the approval of Canadians from coast to coast. Aware that they'd made history, the eleven leaders exchanged hugs and congratulations.

Briefly, the nation applauded. Then the doubts surfaced, in the public and among a number of academics and commentators and some Opposition politicians. Among those critical voices was the voice of Trudeau. He commented that Mulroney had been "a weakling" in yielding to so many provincial demands, above all in conceding to Quebec distinct society status.

Just over one month later, on June 3, the group met again in Ottawa to formally sign their agreement. For the first time, some doubts had begun to penetrate the group itself. As the premier of P.E.I, Joe Giz, later commented, "There was another man in the room that day. We talked about him quite a lot. He was there in spirit. He was Pierre Trudeau."

Mulroney in particular kept dropping Trudeau's name. The meeting took longer than expected. Eventually the leaders assembled to sign the Meech Lake Accord. Its centrepiece was distinct society status for Quebec. The deal still had to be ratified by the federal government and all ten provincial legislatures by June 23, 1990, to make it permanent. This, though, was thought to be only a formality. Every premier had signed the accord. It was, everyone agreed, a done deal.

Then a figure from the past stepped forward and broke the deal in two. Once Pierre Trudeau entered the debate, he did so in the manner that all Canadians remembered so well and for which they had become a little nostalgic; he was fearless, scathing, dismissive, ruthless. "Those Canadians who fought for a single Canada, bilingual and multicultural, can say goodbye to their dreams," he thundered in long statements published simultaneously in the *Toronto Star* newspaper and in Montreal's *La Presse*. Ottawa had lost so much power, he warned, that it would become "a backwater for political and bureaucratic rejects." As for distinct society status, Trudeau said that "Mulroney has put Canada on the fast track for achieving sovereignty-association," or a version of separation. He announced that Mulroney, by giving so much away, would "render the Canadian state totally impotent."

Mulroney repeated again and again that Trudeau's 1982 constitutional deal had "excluded" Quebec. Trudeau considered this an insult, and he neither forgot nor forgave it.

As Trudeau saw it, the dream of a bilingual nation was being betrayed by a grubby compromise. The "balance" that Confederation had maintained between the centre and its regions was being unravelled. This was Trudeau's view. In Mulroney's opinion, though, the concessions he had made to the provinces, most especially to Quebec, were justified by gaining their unanimous consent to the 1982 constitution.

In August 1987 Trudeau came back into public view again. He appeared before the Senate-Commons Committee on the constitution. His performance was electrifying. Dripping scorn and contempt, he said that "we see provincialism developing at the expense of national patriotism." He agreed that Mulroney had negotiated a peace pact with the premiers, but, he went on, "[P]eace at what price? By giving the premiers everything they wanted."

Trudeau had one last chance to address the nation the following March. This time he appeared before the Senate Committee, and there was an elegiac quality to his comments: "We have to realize that Canada is not immortal, but if it is going to go, let it go with a bang rather than a whimper."

He now no longer fought alone. Increasingly, English Canadians showed that they too believed that something irretrievable was being lost, that somehow their dream for Canada was being diminished and sullied. Two provinces, Manitoba and New Brunswick, began demanding changes to the accord. Soon, the newly elected premier of Newfoundland, Clyde Wells, simply refused to accept the deal that Mulroney and the other premiers had negotiated, and successfully enlisted the vast majority of English-speaking Canadians on his side.

In a messy conclusion, the Meech Lake deal finally died in June 1990. There was an attempt to revive it in the form of the Charlottetown Accord, which covered much of the same ground. Trudeau similarly opposed this by issuing what became known as his "Maison de Egg Roll manifesto," based on the name of the Montreal restaurant where he had told friends he intended to intervene in the public debate. The Charlottetown Accord was rejected by Canadians in the national referendum of 1992. Trudeau had won his last fight.

The lion was getting wintry now. Trudeau still walked crisply each day from his house to his office, still travelled, and still read widely. (One of the books he read at this time was the entire Bible.) But he was now entirely out of public affairs. When a second Quebec referendum on separation was held in the fall of 1995, organizers for the federalists specifically asked Trudeau *not* to intervene because organizers for the federalist side worried that Trudeau's involvement might inflame Quebecers and increase the vote for separatism. (As it turned out, the voting results were extremely close; the separatists ended up losing by less than 1 per cent of the votes cast.)

Quebecers rejected him, but other Canadians now embraced Trudeau more fully than they ever had. Kenneth McRoberts, a political scientist and a strong critic of Trudeau, paid Trudeau perhaps the highest political compliment ever accorded to him. It was a "supreme irony," wrote McRoberts, that Trudeau had come to be "embraced by much of English Canada as the 'saviour' of the Canadian nation and ultimately emerges as the champion of Canadian nationalism." Trudeau, the anti-nationalist, thus had become the leader of Canadian nationalists.

Increasingly, Canadians outside of Quebec began to express a new kind of Canadianism that was positive, self-confident, and outward-turned. The great majority of the defining elements of that new Canadianism can be traced directly back to Trudeau. The Charter of Rights and Freedoms that Trudeau had championed was the foundation upon which all else was built. Added to it was the new Canadian commitment to bilingualism, multiculturalism, cultural and racial diversity, regional variety, equality of the provinces, and a humanistic internationalism.

As important to the country, or even more so, was the symbol that Trudeau came to express by his own character. To successive generations of Canadians, he came to personify excellence, both physical and intellectual. Through his example as leader, they came to believe that they, too, and their country, could also be excellent.

The years passed, but Trudeau's allure never died. When he published his memoirs in 1993, reviewers universally panned the book, and yet it sold an all-time record of 150,000 copies. In 2002 a TV mini-series about Trudeau attracted the CBC's largest audiences in the decade. Whenever high school students, all born after Trudeau had left office in 1984, were asked by pollsters to name Canadian heroes, time and again they placed Trudeau at the very top of their list alongside hockey superstar Wayne Gretzky.

Trudeau's last years were painful. His youngest son Michel died at the age of 23 in a skiing accident in British Columbia in November 1998. This loss caused Trudeau to doubt his faith and God's very existence; it was a spiritual crisis he only overcame near the end of his own life.

In 1999 Pierre Trudeau was diagnosed with prostate cancer and refused to have surgery. His funeral on October 3, 2000, was a national event without equal. Huge crowds gathered in silence. Heads were bowed and tears fell as a special train carrying his coffin made its slow way from Ottawa to Montreal, where he was buried. The country suddenly seemed a lot smaller.

Pierre Trudeau's funeral

Political Afterlife and Death

Pierre Trudeau – Timeline

1919	Born on October 18 in Montreal
1931	Becomes a student at Collège Jean de Brébeuf in Montreal
1943	Graduates in law from University of Montreal
1945	Receives masters degree from Harvard in political economy
1947	Attends London School of Economics
1961	Becomes professor of constitutional law at University of Montreal
1965	Elected to Parliament
1967	Becomes minister of justice under Lester Pearson
1968	Becomes leader of the Liberal Party and wins first election
1970	Invokes War Measures Act
1971	Marries Margaret Sinclair
1972	Elected with a minority government
1974	Re-elected with majority government
1976	Bill 22 makes Quebec officially unilingual; Lévesque is elected premier
1977	Trudeau and Margaret divorce
1979	Loses election and becomes Opposition leader
1980	Wins election after Conservatives lose budget vote
1981	All provinces except Quebec sign Charter of Rights and Freedoms
1982	Queen Elizabeth proclaims Canada's new constitution
1984	Resigns as prime minister
1987	Speaks out against Meech Lake Accord
1998	Youngest son Michel dies in avalanche
2000	Dies of cancer on September 28

Further Reading

Christiano, Kevin J. *Pierre Elliott Trudeau: Reason Before Passion*. Toronto: ECW Press, 1995.

Clarkson, Stephen, and Christina McCall. *Trudeau and Our Times, vol. 1 & 2*. Toronto: McClelland & Stewart, 1997.

Gwyn, Richard. *The Northern Magus: Pierre Trudeau and Canadians*. Toronto: McClelland & Stewart, 1980.

Head, Ivan L., and Pierre Elliott Trudeau. *The Canadian Way: Shaping Canada's Foreign Policy, 1968-84*. Toronto: McClelland & Stewart, 1995.

Pelletier, Gérard. *Years of Impatience, 1950-1960*. Toronto: Methuen, 1984.

Southam, Nancy. *Pierre: Colleagues and Friends Talk about the Trudeau They Knew*. Toronto: McClelland & Stewart, 2005.

Stuebing, Douglas. *Trudeau, A Man for Tomorrow*. Toronto: Clarke, Irwin, 1968.

Trudeau, Pierre Elliott, and Thomas Axworthy. *Towards a Just Society: The Trudeau Years*. Toronto: Penguin Books, 2000.

Credits

Index